EASY PEASY!

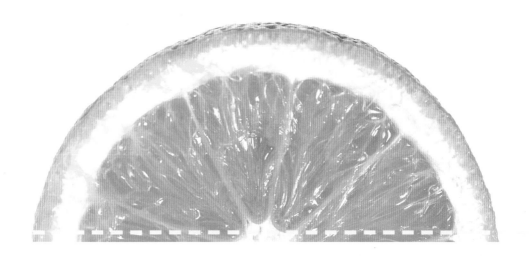

EASY PEASY!

Real Cooking for Kids

MARY CONTINI
AND
PRU IRVINE

First published in 2018 by
BC Books, an imprint of
Birlinn Limited
West Newington House
10 Newington Road
Edinburgh EH9 1QS

www.bcbooksforkids.co.uk

ISBN: 978 1 78027 528 4

British Library
Cataloguing-in-Publication Data
A catalogue record for this book
is available from the British Library

Designed by James Hutcheson
Page make up by Mark Blackadder

Printed and bound by
PNB, Latvia

To my mother, Gertrude,
and my mother, Lyn

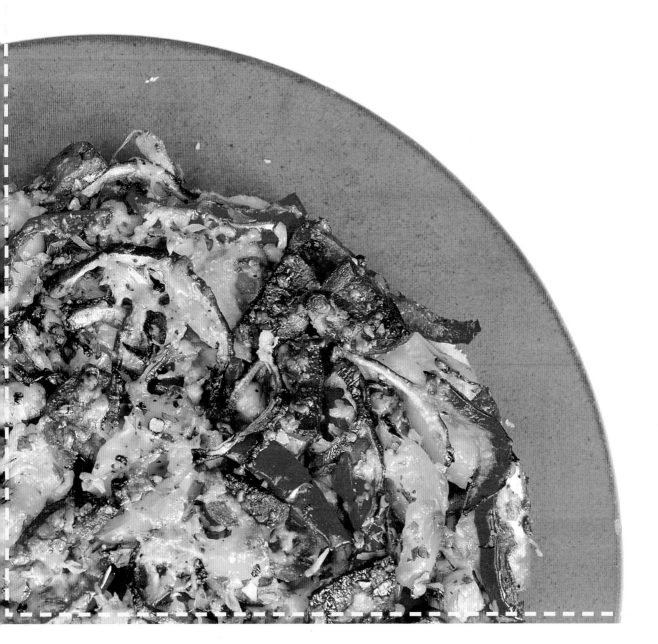

Contents

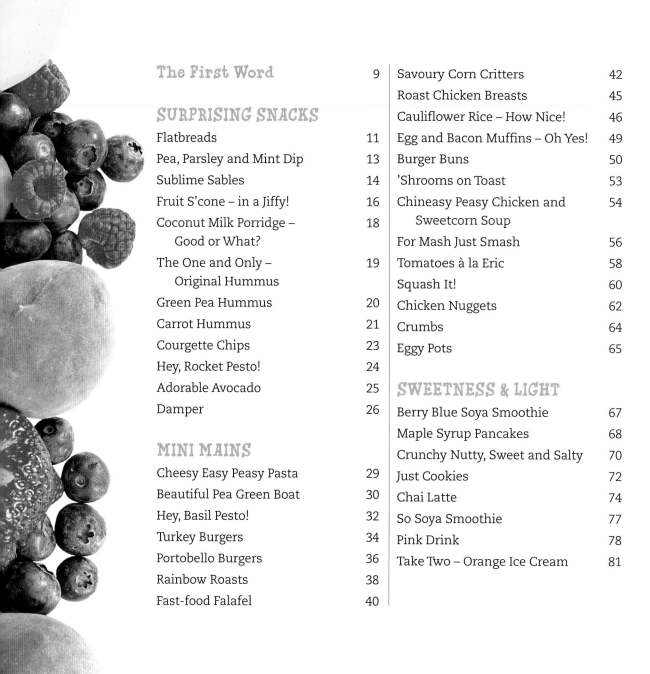

The First Word — 9

SURPRISING SNACKS

Flatbreads — 11
Pea, Parsley and Mint Dip — 13
Sublime Sables — 14
Fruit S'cone – in a Jiffy! — 16
Coconut Milk Porridge –
 Good or What? — 18
The One and Only –
 Original Hummus — 19
Green Pea Hummus — 20
Carrot Hummus — 21
Courgette Chips — 23
Hey, Rocket Pesto! — 24
Adorable Avocado — 25
Damper — 26

MINI MAINS

Cheesy Easy Peasy Pasta — 29
Beautiful Pea Green Boat — 30
Hey, Basil Pesto! — 32
Turkey Burgers — 34
Portobello Burgers — 36
Rainbow Roasts — 38
Fast-food Falafel — 40

Savoury Corn Critters — 42
Roast Chicken Breasts — 45
Cauliflower Rice – How Nice! — 46
Egg and Bacon Muffins – Oh Yes! — 49
Burger Buns — 50
'Shrooms on Toast — 53
Chineasy Peasy Chicken and
 Sweetcorn Soup — 54
For Mash Just Smash — 56
Tomatoes à la Eric — 58
Squash It! — 60
Chicken Nuggets — 62
Crumbs — 64
Eggy Pots — 65

SWEETNESS & LIGHT

Berry Blue Soya Smoothie — 67
Maple Syrup Pancakes — 68
Crunchy Nutty, Sweet and Salty — 70
Just Cookies — 72
Chai Latte — 74
So Soya Smoothie — 77
Pink Drink — 78
Take Two – Orange Ice Cream — 81

SCRUMPTIOUS SALADS

Perfect Peppers	83
Moorish Carrot Salad	84
Feta Complee!	87
Cool as a Cucumber	88
Hail Caesar Salad!	90
Croutons	91

DIVINE DINNERS

Knock-up Tart	93
Tutti Frutti Chicken Curry	94
Spanish Omelette	96
It's a Bit Chilli!	98
Lemon Chicken and Potato Wedges	100
Koftas	102
Rib Ticklers	104
Chow-chow Noodles	106
You're a Nut Burger!	108
Gnocchi	110
S'beans	112
Soo-go	114
Balls in Soo-go	116
Brain Food	119
Over T'ofu!	120
Mozzarella Eggs	121

FABULOUS FRUITS

Granny Smith's Fruit	123
Rhubarb and Banana Fool	124
More Fruits . . .	127
Marvellous Muesli	128
Scrumptious Slappleberry	130

The Knack	131
The Last Word	139
Acknowledgements	140
Index	141

The First Word

The *Easy Peasy* Club is recruiting new members for a cooking and eating journey of our favourite dishes from around the world. You don't need anything except a kitchen and a real love of eating fabulous food. Sound good to you? Sounds OK to us. About 300 years ago we wrote the first *Easy Peasy* books and everyone seemed to like them. So we thought we'd go global and look at foods from everywhere, not just Britain.

Being able to cook your own food is more important than ever now, as the foodies are always on our tails about fat, sugar, salt and a hundred other things we shouldn't be eating. It seems like we're not allowed to enjoy what we eat any more. But take heart, friends! We've been listening to you and have put together a pile of really simple, gorgeous, good-for-you recipes. Once you start this journey with us, we think you'll find it's about a love of cooking and eating and sharing with family and friends. What could be nicer?

Enjoy everything you cook!
With our love,
Easy & Peasy xxx

Psst! Anything marked with ☺ is explained in The Knack at the back of the book. This is the place to discover how to do things, like chop an onion, peel and slice. Or, if you're having a truly exotic kitchen moment, it'll even tell you how to stone a mango!!

Pssst! All our recipes are for four people, unless we say otherwise.

Surprising Snacks

FLATBREADS

Flatbreads are fabulous. Fabulously easy to make, fabulously easy to eat. And you'll feel fabulously proud when friends marvel at your genius in the kitchen. Although they originally come from Ancient Egypt, most countries have their own version. It is, after all, just a *flat* bread!

What do bakers give their friends on special occasions? Flours!

READY . . .

250g of plain flour
1 teaspoon of sea salt
1 tablespoon of olive oil
150ml of warm water

. . . .

a medium bowl
a rolling pin
a non-stick frying pan or griddle
cling film
a spatula or tongs

STEADY . . .

- Get all your ingredients ready.

GO!

1. Put the flour, sea salt, oil and water into the bowl. Mix together with your hands.
2. Tip the dough onto a lightly floured work surface or board. Knead for a few minutes.
3. Roll it into a ball, cover with cling film and leave for about 15–20 minutes.
4. Divide the dough into 8 balls and roll each one on the floured surface into a nice thin round. It doesn't have to be perfect, but it does have to be thin!
5. Heat the frying pan or griddle and when it's really hot place a flatbread into the pan. Leave it for about 2 minutes. When you see dark spots on the underside, use the spatula or tongs to turn it over and give it another minute or so. Take it off the heat.
6. Keep doing that until you've used up all the dough.
7. If you plan to eat the flatbreads immediately, keep them warm inside a tea towel until they're all ready.

Psst!

- These are divine with hummus and dips, or Adorable Avocado (p. 25), Fast-food Falafel (p. 40) or It's a Bit Chilli! (p. 98).
- If you like the idea of garlic flatbreads, then brush each flatbread with some garlic oil before putting it into the hot pan. To make the oil, add some thin slices of garlic to a small bottle of olive oil. Screw on the lid and leave for several hours so the flavours develop. You can keep topping up the oil and it should last for months.
- If you're not eating them straight away, brush them with a little oil and refresh them in a hot oven (200°C/Gas mark 6) for a few minutes to make them crisp.

PEA, PARSLEY AND MINT DIP

We bet you don't know what happens to peas when they meet parsley, mint and a few other friends in the food processor. Well, try this and you'll find out! The trick is to get the right balance between the sour lemon and the sweet peas. You'll know when it's right. Trust your tastes.

What do vegetables want more than anything else?
Peas on earth!

READY . . .

250g of frozen peas
½ a small red onion
20g of flat leaf parsley
20g of fresh mint leaves
4–5 tablespoons of olive oil
the juice of half a lemon
a good pinch of both sea salt and
     black pepper

. . . .

a chopping board & sharp knife
a small saucepan
a colander
a food processor
a medium bowl

STEADY . . .

- Get all your ingredients ready.
- Cook the peas for approximately 5–6 minutes, following the instructions on the bag, then drain them in a colander. Refresh them under cold running water, as this keeps them nice and green.
- Peel and chop the onion, any old how,° and roughly chop the herbs.

GO!

1. Put all the ingredients into the food processor and whizz until you have a texture you like – lumpy or smooth.
2. Taste it, and add more salt or pepper and/or lemon juice if it needs it.

Psst!

- It's pretty good on its own but try it with Flatbreads (p. 11) and feel the lurve!
- Freezes perfectly in an airtight container.

13

SUBLIME SABLES

What is a sable, we hear you ask? It's either a dark brown furry animal or it's a sublime, delicate, crumbly 'cookie' from the Normandy region of France. It's both! But we've decided to cook the cookie not the animal. OK with you? These little biscuits will dissolve on your tongue into a soft, cheesy melting moment.

READY . . .

80g of strong white flour
80g of butter, cold from the fridge
80g of grated Parmesan or strong
　　cheddar
a pinch of cayenne pepper
a pinch of sea salt

• • • •

a chopping board & sharp knife
a food processor
weighing scales

cling film
a non-stick or lined baking tray
a cooling rack

STEADY . . .

- Turn on the oven to 180°C/Gas mark 4.
- Get all your ingredients ready.
- Cut the butter into chunks.

GO!

1. Put all the ingredients into your food processor and whizz until it forms a lump.
2. Scatter a little flour on your work surface and tip the dough onto it.
3. Using your hands, mould it into a sausage shape, wrap it up in cling film and pop it in the freezer.
4. Take it out after 30 minutes and slice it into thin rounds, then place these on the baking tray – allow some room between them because they'll spread a bit.
5. Cook for 13–15 minutes until they're golden.
6. Carefully remove the baking tray and arrange the biscuits on the cooling rack. Let them go cold before you tuck in!

Psst!

- The brilliant thing about sable dough is that you can leave it in the freezer until you want it, so you'll always have some ready to slice and bake.
- Once they're cooked and cold, you can store them in an airtight container until they go soft – a week or more even.

15

FRUIT S'CONE - IN A JIFFY!

Scones are great because the quicker you make them, the lighter they are. The lighter they are, the faster you can eat them. This is one recipe where practice really does make perfect. So keep practising!

READY . . .

225g of self-raising flour, plus a little extra for dusting
1 tablespoon of caster sugar
a pinch of sea salt
2 tablespoons of sultanas
50g of soft butter
1 free-range egg
150ml of milk

. . . .

a medium-sized bowl
a small bowl
weighing scales
a sieve
a 3cm cookie cutter – larger or smaller, if you want
a non-stick or lined baking tray

STEADY . . .

- Turn on the oven to 220°C/Gas mark 7.
- Get all your ingredients ready.

GO!

1. Sieve the flour into the medium-sized bowl, then add the sugar, salt, sultanas and butter. Rub the mixture between your fingers as quickly and as lightly as you can to incorporate the flour.
2. In the small bowl, beat the egg with the milk and add to the flour mixture. Use a knife to mix it into a dough. It should only take 2–3 minutes (you may find using your hands easier, and you could also do it in a food processor – it'll take just seconds).
3. Sprinkle some flour onto a clean work surface and your hands. Tip the dough out and lightly flatten it into a round, about 3cm deep.

4. Dip the cookie cutter into some flour, then press it into the dough mix. Tap the scone from the cutter onto your hand and then put it on the baking tray. Carry on until it's all used up. You'll need to gently re-roll some bits as you go.

5. Dust the scones with a little flour or brush them with a little milk or some beaten egg.

6. Put them into the oven for 10–12 minutes until they're risen and slightly golden on top.

7. Serve while still warm with jam, butter or clotted cream.

Psst!

- If you make smaller scones, then bake them a little less; for bigger scones, bake them a little more.
- If you want a *plain scone*, just leave out the sultanas. If you want a *cheese scone*, add a handful of grated cheddar into the mix and maybe a sprinkling on top.
- They'll keep for a few days in an airtight container, but they freeze perfectly. Remember to warm them up in the oven after defrosting.
- You can freeze these *before* you cook them as well, after you've cut them out. Just defrost them 10 minutes before you bake them.

COCONUT MILK PORRIDGE – GOOD OR WHAT?

Porridge is an anytime, any meal dish – not just for breakfast. Pru's mum eats hers with cream, but she's 92, so anything goes. This is a fabulous porridge – it's full of good-for-you ingredients and incredibly delicious.

READY . . .

300ml of coconut milk
300ml of water
1 teaspoon of ground cardamom
100g of porridge oats
1 teaspoon of vanilla extract
1 ripe mango and/or a banana
runny honey

• • • •

a chopping board & sharp knife
weighing scales
a small saucepan

STEADY . . .

- Get all your ingredients ready.
- Peel and chop the mango☺ and set aside.

GO!

1. Put the coconut milk, water and ground cardamom into the saucepan and bring to the boil.
2. Add the porridge oats and vanilla extract and give it a good stir. Turn the heat to low and let it cook for about 10 minutes, stirring a few times until the oats are soft and the porridge is thick.
3. Pour it into bowls, pile on the fruit and a drizzle of runny honey.

Psst!

- You can also microwave this for 3–4 minutes on full power. Stir it halfway through.

THE ONE AND ONLY – ORIGINAL HUMMUS

Hummus is a delicious, creamy dip of chickpeas, olive oil, garlic and lemon, and it has been enjoyed for centuries as an everyday food in Middle Eastern and North African countries. Making your own is like a badge of honour. It tastes a hundred-million times better than the shop-bought kind. You think we exaggerate? We don't think so!

READY . . .

1 tin of chickpeas
1 large clove of garlic, or 2 smaller ones
1 tablespoon of tahini (sesame seed paste)
1 large pinch of sea salt
the juice of half a lemon

. . . .

a chopping board & sharp knife
a colander
a blender or food processor

STEADY . . .

- Get all your ingredients ready.
- Drain the chickpeas in the colander.
- Peel the garlic.

GO!

1. Put all the ingredients into the blender or food processor and whizz until you get a texture you like. Hummus is normally quite smooth.
2. Taste it! Hummus can be bland, so add more salt or lemon if you think it needs it. And if it's a bit thick, add a glug of olive oil or a tablespoon of water.

Psst!

- Serve this with Flatbreads (p. 11).
- For a real feast, make this with Green Pea Hummus (p. 20) and some Fast-food Falafel (p. 40). Add pitta breads and serve for lunch with a tomato salad. Gorgeous!

GREEN PEA HUMMUS

Hummus is usually made with chickpeas, but there's no reason why we should always use them. The word hummus is actually Arabic for 'chickpeas' and that's where it came from first. Today you'll find all different kinds of hummus – here is another option for you to try.

READY ...

500g of frozen petit pois
2 tablespoons of tahini (sesame seed paste)
the juice of a large lemon
3 tablespoons of extra virgin olive oil
2 large cloves of garlic
1 teaspoon of ground cumin
a large handful of parsley
a large pinch each of sea salt and black pepper

• • • •

a chopping board & sharp knife
a medium-sized saucepan
a colander
a food processor

STEADY ...

- Get all your ingredients ready.
- Peel the garlic.☺
- Cook the peas for 5–6 minutes, as instructed on the packet. Drain them and refresh under cold running water, as this keeps them nice and green.

GO!

1. Tip the peas into the food processor.
2. Add the rest of the ingredients and whizz, but not too much as you want a bit of texture. If you think it's a bit thick, add a drop of water to loosen it up.
3. Taste it and add a little more sea salt, pepper and/or oil until it tastes scrummy.

Psst!

- This is divine served with Flatbreads (p. 11).
- Put it in an airtight container and it'll keep in the fridge for a couple of days.
- It freezes really well too!

CARROT HUMMUS

What's orange and sounds like 'parrot'? Carrot! OK, it wasn't funny, but we tried. Now you can try hummus No. 3. Just imagine how incredible it would be to have a bright green bowl of Green Pea Hummus alongside a wild orange bowl of Carrot Hummus. Nobody could resist either you or your hummus!

READY . . .

1 teaspoon of ground cumin
1 teaspoon of ground coriander
3 tablespoons of olive oil
3 large cloves of garlic
500g of carrots
sea salt and black pepper
the juice of half an orange, or 50ml of
    fresh orange juice
the juice of half a lemon, or 20ml of
    lemon juice
2 tablespoons of either smooth
    peanut butter or tahini paste

. . . .

a chopping board & sharp knife
weighing scales
mixing bowl
a non-stick or lined baking tray
food processor

STEADY . . .

- Turn on the oven to 200°C/Gas mark 6.
- Get all your ingredients ready.
- Put the spices and olive oil into your mixing bowl.
- Peel and chop the garlic☺ and add it to the bowl.
- Peel, wash and chop the carrots, any old how.☺
- Add a big pinch of sea salt and black pepper.
- Mix the whole lot together.

GO!

1. Tip the mixture onto the lined baking tray and roast for 25 minutes.
2. Using oven gloves, carefully take it out of the oven and let it cool for a few minutes.
3. Now tip the carrots into your food processor.
4. Add the orange and lemon juice, and the peanut butter or tahini paste.
5. Whizz it until you get a texture you like – either very soft or a bit lumpy.
6. Put it into a bowl and let it go cold. Taste it and add more seasoning or lemon juice, if you think it needs it.

Psst!

- Like the Green Pea Hummus (p. 20), this is gorgeous with Flatbreads (p. 11) or anything else you want to dip into it – fingers, breadsticks, pitta breads, whatever!

COURGETTE CHIPS

Here's a thing – a green chip! Go on, try it! You know you want to . . .

READY . . .
1–2 free-range eggs
sea salt and black pepper
6–8 large courgettes
5–6 tablespoons of plain flour
100ml of sunflower oil

. . . .

a chopping board & sharp knife
a small bowl
a large plate
a sieve
a shallow frying pan
a spatula
a slotted spoon
kitchen paper

STEADY . . .
- Get all your ingredients ready.
- Wash the courgettes and trim off the ends. Cut them into long chip shapes. Pat them dry on kitchen paper to remove as much moisture as possible.
- Break the eggs into the bowl,☺ add some sea salt and black pepper and whisk well with a fork.
- Sieve the flour onto a plate and season it with some sea salt and black pepper.

GO!
1. Roll the courgette chips around in the flour.
2. Warm the oil in the frying pan on a medium heat and add one green chip carefully. Hot oil can splash! When it starts to sizzle, dip the others into the beaten egg and put them, a few at a time, into the frying pan.
3. Turn them with a spatula so they cook on each side. They're ready when they stop sizzling.
4. Remove them from the frying pan with a slotted spoon, drain them on some kitchen paper and keep them warm until you're ready to eat.

23

HEY, ROCKET PESTO!

Have you ever tasted bought pesto from a jar, screwed up your nose and pretended to gag? Well, never again. Here's the one for you. Dead simple, dead gorgeous and works with everything from pasta and potatoes to fish and tomatoes. Be brave, be adventurous. Dive in!

READY . . .

1 large or 2 small cloves of garlic
120g of rocket, spinach & watercress
  salad
3 tablespoons of pine nuts
150ml of extra virgin olive oil
a large pinch of sea salt
½ a lemon
60g of grated Parmesan cheese

. . . .

a chopping board & sharp knife
weighing scales
a grater
a medium bowl
a food processor

STEADY . . .

- Get all your ingredients ready.
- Peel the garlic. ☺
- Toast the pine nuts, being careful not to burn them. ☺

GO!

1. Tip the whole lot – except the cheese and the lemon – into the food processor and whizz until it's good and saucy. You might need a spatula to push it down the sides every now and then.
2. Tip it into the bowl and add the cheese. Mix thoroughly.
3. Taste it and add a squeeze of lemon juice, ☺ and some more salt if it needs it.

Psst!

- It'll keep in the fridge for a couple of weeks in a jar or airtight container.
- It freezes brilliantly. Pop it into a few small airtight containers so you've got several meals ready and waiting. Remember to defrost it before using.

ADORABLE AVOCADO

When the British first saw avocados in South America they called them 'alligator pears' because they had a rough green skin and looked like an odd-shaped pear. They are bang on good for you, taste delicious and are packed with protein. You know they're ripe when they feel heavy in your hand and the top is slightly soft when you press it gently.

Be very careful when you open an avocado. There's a new injury called 'avocado hand' where people try to open the fruit the wrong way and stab themselves.

READY . . .

2 ripe avocados
1 lime, or half a lemon
a good size bunch of fresh coriander
    leaves
½ a red onion
3 cherry tomatoes
Tabasco sauce
sea salt

. . . .

a chopping board & sharp knife
a mixing bowl

STEADY . . . & GO!

1. Get all your ingredients ready.
2. Scoop the flesh of the avocados⊙ into the mixing bowl.
3. Add the juice of the lime or lemon⊙ and mash with a fork until it's as soft and mushy as you like.
4. Chop up the coriander and add it to the bowl.
5. Slice the onion⊙ and tomatoes as finely as you can and add them too.
6. Now add a few drops of Tabasco and some sea salt.
7. Mix it all together very gently, taste it and add more salt, Tabasco or lime/lemon, if you think it needs it.

Psst!

- This is best eaten fresh, but if you cover it with a teaspoon of olive oil and some cling film it will stop it going brown. It won't last much more than a day in the fridge.
- Pile it into a wrap or Flatbread (p. 11), or eat it with It's a Bit Chilli (p. 98). Very scrummy with Turkey Burgers (p. 34) as well. And not bad with crisps or tortilla chips either!

DAMPER

Dampers are Australian soda breads. What is a soda bread, we hear you ask? Well, it's bread made without yeast and so it takes minutes, not hours, to make. Have you got some minutes? Then let's make it!

Dampers were originally cooked by swagmen, drovers, stockmen and other travellers who roamed the Outback. They were baked in the coals of a campfire and eaten with dried or cooked meat, or golden syrup. What's not to like? While you are waiting for it to cook, look up the meaning of the word 'swagman'. You'll have a laugh!

READY . . .

450g of self-raising flour
40g of butter
1 tablespoon of caster sugar
1 teaspoon of sea salt
250ml of milk

. . . .

a chopping board & sharp knife
weighing scales
a large bowl
a food processor
a non-stick or
    lined baking
    tray

STEADY . . .

- Turn on the oven to 200°C/Gas mark 6.
- Get all your ingredients ready.

GO!

1. Put the flour, butter, sugar and salt into the food processor and whizz a few times until you've got crumbs.

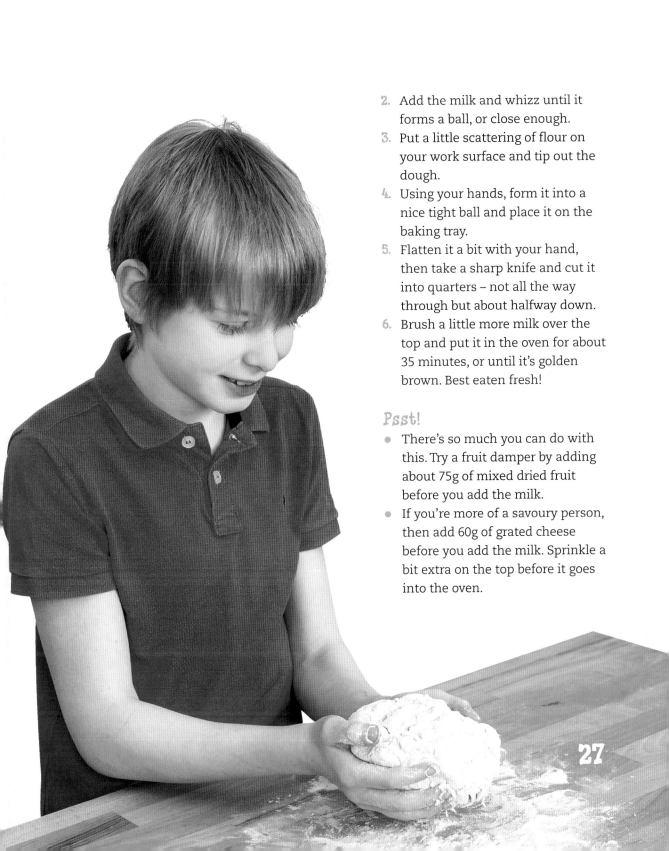

2. Add the milk and whizz until it forms a ball, or close enough.
3. Put a little scattering of flour on your work surface and tip out the dough.
4. Using your hands, form it into a nice tight ball and place it on the baking tray.
5. Flatten it a bit with your hand, then take a sharp knife and cut it into quarters – not all the way through but about halfway down.
6. Brush a little more milk over the top and put it in the oven for about 35 minutes, or until it's golden brown. Best eaten fresh!

Psst!

- There's so much you can do with this. Try a fruit damper by adding about 75g of mixed dried fruit before you add the milk.
- If you're more of a savoury person, then add 60g of grated cheese before you add the milk. Sprinkle a bit extra on the top before it goes into the oven.

27

Mini Mains

CHEESY EASY PEASY PASTA

This soft and gooey pasta is too easy to make and too easy to eat. Just the thing if you want a quick supper in front of the telly.

READY ...

300g of pasta – any shape you want
a large blob of butter
160g of grated Parmesan or cheddar,
    plus a bit extra for the top
some sea salt and black pepper

• • • •

a large saucepan
weighing scales
a colander

STEADY ...

- Get all your ingredients ready.
- First, cook the pasta.☺ Drain it in the colander in the sink and then tip it back into the cooking pot.

GO!

1. Add the butter, cheese and some sea salt and black pepper to the pasta. Mix it all together until the cheese has melted.
2. Serve it with an extra sprinkling of cheese on top.

Psst!

- This can be a great *Easy Peasy* meal for one – just use 75g of pasta, 40g of cheese and a small blob of butter!

BEAUTIFUL PEA GREEN BOAT

'The owl and the pussy cat went to sea in a beautiful pea green boat' – and ate it! How about making an *Easy Peasy* pot of homemade soup?

READY . . .

50g of butter
1 onion
180g of smoked lardons (bacon bits)
1 litre of water
450g of frozen peas
sea salt and black pepper
2 sprigs of fresh mint

. . . .

a chopping board & sharp knife
a medium-sized saucepan with a lid
a food processor

STEADY . . .

- Get all your ingredients ready.
- Peel and chop the onion any old how.☺

GO!

1. Melt the butter in the saucepan over a medium heat and add the onion.
2. Stir the onion around in the butter, then lower the heat, put the lid on and let it cook slowly until it's soft – about 10 minutes.
3. Raise the heat and add the lardons, stirring them around in the onion until golden and browned.
4. Now add the water, bring to the boil and simmer☺ for about 20 minutes with the lid on.
5. Add the frozen peas, bring back to a simmer and cook for 5 minutes.
6. Add a good pinch of sea salt and pepper.

7. Carefully ladle or pour the soup into the food processor and whizz a few times. It can be thick and lumpy or smooth and silky, whatever takes your fancy.

8. Pour the soup back into the saucepan and reheat it. Add the mint and more water if you think it is too thick.

9. Taste it and add more sea salt or pepper if it needs it.

10. Serve it with some chopped mint.

Psst!

● Serve the soup with a blob of crème fraîche for extra gorgeousness!

● You can scatter a handful of Croutons (p. 91) over the soup just before serving.

● You can make this without the bacon, but use 1 litre of vegetable stock instead of water.

HEY, BASIL PESTO!

If you're not quite brave enough yet for Hey, Rocket Pesto!, then try the original pesto first. This was the one we had as children before someone discovered there could be loads of different kinds, we'd just never thought of them! So if you want to become 'Pesto Friends' with all your mates, try this mixed through a steaming bowl of spaghetti topped with Parmesan cheese. Oh my! Pesto heaven . . .

READY . . .

120–135ml of olive oil
100g of fresh basil
2 large cloves of garlic
2 tablespoons of pine nuts
a large pinch of sea salt
50g of grated Parmesan cheese

. . . .

a chopping board & sharp knife
a food processor
a grater
a small serving bowl

STEADY . . .

- Get all your ingredients ready.
- Peel the garlic° and chop the basil.
- Grate the cheese.

GO!

1. Start with 120ml of olive oil and put everything – except the cheese – into the food processor. Whizz until you have a smooth puree. If it looks a bit thick, add a little more oil.
2. Tip it into the serving bowl and gently stir in the cheese.
3. Taste it and add more salt, oil or cheese until it tastes perfect for you.

Psst!

- It'll keep in the fridge for a couple of weeks in a jar or airtight container.
- It also freezes brilliantly. Pop it into a few small, airtight containers so you've got several portions ready and waiting; you'll just need to cook some pasta.

TURKEY BURGERS

The thing is, we all think of turkey as a Christmas treat with lashings of gravy and crispy skin and chipolata sausages. But in fact turkey should be enjoyed all year round. These burgers are extra yummy with the lemon and coriander flavours, which actually make them taste a bit Turkish.

READY . . .

500g of turkey mince
2 teaspoons of ground cumin
2 teaspoons of ground coriander
a large handful of fresh coriander
the juice of half a lemon
sea salt and black pepper
vegetable oil, for frying

. . . .

a chopping board & sharp knife
a mixing bowl
a large frying pan
a non-stick or lined baking tray

STEADY . . .

- Turn on the oven to 200°C/Gas mark 6.
- Get all your ingredients ready.
- Chop up the fresh coriander leaves, as small as you can.

GO!

1. Put everything, *except the oil*, into the mixing bowl and get mixing. Use your hands to mix everything really well. The more you mix, the better the burgers will stay together. It's a bit like kneading dough!

2. When it's the right texture, form 6–8 balls, which you can then flatten into burger shapes.
3. Add the oil to the frying pan and, when it's quite hot, carefully add the burgers. Turn down the heat a little and let them brown for about 3 minutes on each side.
4. Now, transfer the burgers to the baking tray and cook for 15 minutes in the oven.

Psst!

- These are gorgeous with Perfect Peppers (p. 83) and Adorable Avocado (p. 25).
- Turkey burgers can be frozen, but they must be defrosted before going into the oven at 200°C/Gas mark 6 for 15 minutes.

35

PORTOBELLO BURGERS

Mushrooms are sometimes referred to as the 'meat' of the vegetable world. In fact, when they are cooked like this they're so soft and juicy they can be even tastier than meat.

READY . . .

4 Portobello mushrooms
100g of butter
1 large clove of garlic
a small bunch of chopped flat leaf
   parsley
sea salt and black pepper
4 burger buns
4 cheese slices – cheddar, Emmental
   or Gruyère
2 large tomatoes

• • • •

a chopping board & sharp knife
garlic crusher or grater
2 non-stick or lined baking trays
a medium-sized bowl

STEADY . . .

- Turn on the oven to 180°C/Gas mark 4.
- Get all your ingredients ready.
- Trim the stalks of the mushrooms and wipe them clean with a piece of damp kitchen paper.
- Crush the garlic.☺
- Slice the tomatoes, quite thickly.

GO!

1. Lay the mushrooms cap side down (or stalk side up!) on the baking tray.
2. Mash the butter, garlic and parsley together in the bowl and add some sea salt and black pepper.
3. Divide the herby butter equally between the mushrooms.

4. Bake in the oven for 30 minutes.
5. After 20 minutes open the buns and lay them on the second baking tray. Place a cheese slice and some tomato on each bun and put them into the oven with the mushrooms for the last 10 minutes.
6. Carefully take out the buns and the mushrooms and place one mushroom into each bun. Close the bun and dig in!

Psst!

- You can add all sorts of extra fillings – lettuce leaves, pickles, gherkins.
- You could even try stuffing the mushrooms with some garlicky breadcrumbs. See Crumbs (p. 64), and just mix them together with some crushed garlic and melted butter. *Easy Peasy!*

RAINBOW ROASTS

At the end of this rainbow you may not find a pot of gold, but a plate of sweet and soft rainbow roasts is not a bad second best. It's also a quick and easy way to cook and eat a variety of different vegetables, all of them sweet and sticky. And you can eat them with your fingers!

READY . . .

2 large carrots
2 raw beetroots
2 large parsnips
2–3 tablespoons of olive oil
2 teaspoons of cayenne pepper
   or paprika
sea salt

. . . .

a chopping board & sharp knife
a potato peeler
a large bowl
a non-stick or lined baking tray

STEADY . . .

- Turn on the oven to 200°C/ Gas mark 6.
- Get all your ingredients ready.
- Wash, peel and slice all the vegetables so they look like chips.

GO!

1. Pile the sliced vegetables into the bowl and add the oil, cayenne/paprika and a large pinch of sea salt.
2. Mix them all together very thoroughly and empty out onto the baking tray. Try and arrange them in a single layer so they all cook at the same time.
3. Put them into the oven for around 40 minutes, or until they're getting brown around the edges. Check them after half an hour.

Psst!

- Beware the pink juice from beetroot! Don't worry, it won't stain.
- You can always add a potato into the mix.
- These are just as delicious cold. Good for lunchboxes!

39

FAST-FOOD FALAFEL

Long before burgers, chips and pizza, we had falafel. Yeah, it's true! Falafels are a street food from the Middle East. They taste great and are pretty good for you too, bursting with fibre and proteins. They're also a great vegetarian option.

READY . . .

1 tin of chickpeas
1 onion
2 cloves of garlic
a large handful of flat leaf parsley
a small pinch of dried chilli flakes
1 teaspoon of ground coriander
1 teaspoon of cumin
sea salt
vegetable oil, for frying

● ● ● ●

a chopping board & sharp knife
a colander
a food processor
a medium-sized bowl
a large, deep frying pan
kitchen paper

STEADY . . .

● Get all your ingredients ready.
● Drain the chickpeas in the colander and rinse with cold water.
● Peel the onion and slice it thickly. ◎
● Peel the garlic. ◎

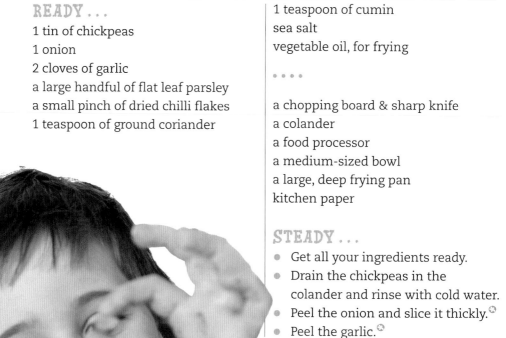

GO!

1. Put all the ingredients – except the oil – into the food processor and whizz until it's still a bit lumpy but holds together when you squeeze a ball of it in your hands.
2. Tip it into the bowl and roll small balls of mixture in your hands. Put them onto the chopping board and flatten them slightly so they're patties rather than balls.
3. Cover the base of the frying pan with vegetable oil (about 2cm deep) and heat. Drop a tiny bit of the mixture into the oil – when it sizzles, it's ready!
4. Very carefully, place the patties into the hot oil using a spatula or kitchen spoon. Fry them until they're lovely and brown, 3–5 minutes.
5. Drain them on kitchen paper and serve hot or cold.

Psst!

- Try these with Moorish Carrot Salad (p. 84) or Green Pea Hummus (p. 20).
- Gorgeous with Flatbreads (p. 11) too.
- They freeze brilliantly but remember to defrost them before warming through in the oven.

SAVOURY CORN CRITTERS

Here's a riddle for you. You throw away the outside, cook the inside, then eat the outside and throw away the inside. What am I?*

 We love these – hot or cold, on their own or with other things. You can make them big or small, you choose, they're your critters!

READY . . .

2 free-range eggs
2 tablespoons of milk
2 tablespoons of self-raising flour
1 small tin of sweetcorn, drained
2 tablespoons of soy sauce
sea salt and black pepper
4–5 spring onions
vegetable oil, for frying

. . . .

a chopping board & sharp knife
a medium-sized bowl
a whisk, or fork
a non-stick frying pan
a spatula

STEADY . . .

- Get all your ingredients ready.
- Prepare the spring onions and slice, as best you can, into thin strips.○

GO!

1. Break the eggs into the bowl○ and add the milk and flour. Whisk it thoroughly until most of the lumps have gone.

2. Add the sweetcorn, soy sauce and a good pinch of sea salt and pepper.
3. Heat a tablespoon of oil in the frying pan and add the spring onions. Let them cook until they're soft, stirring often. Add them to the egg mixture.
4. Now, heat four tablespoons of oil in the frying pan until hot. Drop a tiny bit of the egg mixture into the pan. If it sizzles, it's ready.
5. Put three separate tablespoons of the mixture into the pan, to make three critters. Cook them until they're going brown on the bottom, then using a spatula turn them over and cook the other side for a minute or two.
6. Drain them on kitchen paper and keep them warm while you make the rest.

Psst!

- They are great in a lunchbox. Nice in a sandwich too!

*corn on the cob

ROAST CHICKEN BREASTS

It's so *Easy Peasy* to make delicious roast chicken! This is lovely hot or cold.

READY...

4 free-range chicken breasts, with or without skin
2–3 tablespoons of olive oil
sea salt and black pepper
the juice of half a lemon

a chopping board & sharp knife
an ovenproof dish

STEADY...

- Turn on the oven to 180°C/Gas mark 4.
- Get all your ingredients ready.

GO!

1. Put the chicken into the ovenproof dish and rub the oil over them. Remember to wash your hands afterwards!
2. Sprinkle with sea salt and a few grindings of black pepper.
3. Put in the oven and roast for 30–40 minutes.
4. When you take them out, slice one of them in the middle to check there's no pink meat inside.☺ If there is, pop it back into the oven for another 5–10 minutes.
5. Squeeze over the lemon juice.☺

Psst!

- Use these for Hail Caesar Salad (p. 90), and they are scrummy with Perfect Peppers (p. 83) and Adorable Avocado (p. 25). Or pile them into a Flatbread (p. 11) with any of the above.

CAULIFLOWER RICE – HOW NICE!

We're deadly serious when we say this is really scrummy! We know you 'HATE' cauliflower, but you've no idea what a taste sensation you'll miss if you don't try this. Just ask yourself: What do you get if you cross a dog with a daffodil? A collieflower! Oh, by the way, cauliflower is so packed with vitamins and minerals that it'll soon be called a 'superfood'!

READY . . .

1 small cauliflower
a large blob of butter
1 tablespoon of olive oil
a large pinch of sea salt
a large handful of parsley
60–70g of flaked almonds
plenty of grated Parmesan or cheddar

. . . .

a chopping board & sharp knife
a food processor
a medium-sized frying pan with a lid
a grater

STEADY . . .

- Get all your ingredients ready.
- Cut the leaves off the cauliflower and break into florets. Throw away any chunks of stalk.
- Chop the parsley as finely as you can.
- Toast the almonds, being careful not to burn them.☺

GO!

1. Put the florets into the food processor and whizz a few times until the cauliflower looks like rice.
2. Melt the butter and oil in the frying pan until the butter starts to make sizzling sounds.
3. Add the cauliflower rice and mix it through. Lower the heat, put the lid on and cook for about 5 minutes, giving it a stir occasionally.
4. Now add the parsley, salt and almonds, and mix through.

5. Continue cooking for another 4–5 minutes until it's as soft as you like it.
6. Serve with lashings of cheese!

Psst!

- There are lots of fab flavours you can combine with cauliflower rice. Instead of almonds and parsley, try a tablespoon of toasted cumin seeds and fresh, chopped coriander.
- You can even roast it on 180°C/Gas mark 4 for around 25 minutes. Just put the cauliflower, parsley and a clove of peeled garlic into the processor and whizz. Mix it together with 2–3 tablespoons of olive oil, tip it onto a roasting tray and stick it in the oven. Serve drizzled with lemon juice and some more parsley.
- There's also a microwave option. Do all the whizzing in the food processor, but then cover with cling film, pierce the top a few times and cook on full power for 5–7 minutes, or until it's as cooked as you like.

EGG AND BACON MUFFINS – OH YES!

Do not laugh! Muffins don't have to be made with blueberries. You can have savoury ones, too. And what better way to have eggs, bacon and cheese than in a muffin that you can eat with your fingers, take to school or college, or even eat in bed! Better than a big fry-up any day.

READY . . .

180g of lardons (bacon bits) – smoked or not; whichever you prefer
75g of plain flour
1 teaspoon of baking powder
1 teaspoon of mustard powder
75g of strong cheddar, grated
75g of butter
2 large free-range eggs
110g of crème frâiche

. . . .

a small non-stick frying pan
weighing scales
a grater
2 mixing bowls
a whisk, or fork
a muffin tray, or muffin cases

STEADY . . .

- Turn on the oven to 190°C/Gas mark 5.
- Get all your ingredients ready.

GO!

1. Heat the frying pan until it's hot, then fry your lardons until they're crisp. Let them drain on some kitchen paper.
2. Sift the flour, baking powder and mustard powder into a bowl and add the lardons and grated cheese.
3. Melt the butter☺ and add it to the mixture.
4. In the other bowl, whisk the eggs and crème frâiche and add them to the mixture.
5. Stir it gently and carefully so it's well mixed, but ignore the lumps.
6. Spoon the mixture carefully into the muffin tray/cases. Place in the oven and cook for 15 minutes.
7. Serve them warm, but they are delicious cold.

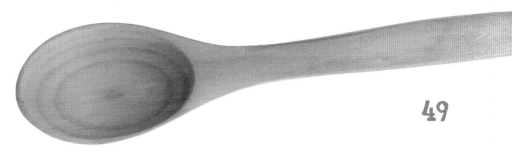

BURGER BUNS

Come on, friends, it's so easy to make burgers just the way you like them. Choose the best lean mince for the nicest taste. This is a basic burger recipe, but there are endless varieties and endless ways to serve them.

READY . . .

500g of lean minced beef
sea salt and black pepper
a good splash of Worcestershire sauce
2 tablespoons of vegetable oil
6 burger buns

. . . .

a medium-sized bowl
a medium-sized frying pan
a spatula

STEADY . . .

- Get all your ingredients ready.
- Put the beef into the bowl and season it with the sea salt, black pepper and Worcestershire sauce. Mix it all together with your hands very thoroughly – squidging and squeezing so it starts to stick together.
- Divide the mixture into 6 balls and squash them into burger shapes.

GO!

1. Warm the oil in the frying pan. Drop a tiny bit of the mixture into the oil and when it starts to fizz a little it's ready.
2. Add the burgers in one layer and cook them over a medium heat until they've browned and crisped on one side.
3. Using the spatula, turn them over and keep them on the heat until they're cooked right through – about 10–15 minutes in total. Check they're ready by cutting through one and making sure there's no pink meat in the middle.
4. Pop them into the burger buns and go for it!

Psst!

- If you want to jazz them up, try adding some cheese slices on top of the burgers for the last few minutes of cooking. Just scrape all the delicious goo onto the burger bun. You can add slices of seasoned tomatoes and lettuce as well. Even gherkins or pickles!
- These burgers will freeze brilliantly, but remember to wrap them individually in the freezer bag otherwise they'll all stick together. When you are ready to cook them again, defrost them first and pop them into a hot oven – 200°C/Gas mark 6 – for about 10 minutes.

'SHROOMS ON TOAST

Cooking mushrooms like this, with olive oil, garlic, chilli and parsley, transforms them into a very satisfying meal.

Why did the mushroom feel left out?
He was always kept in the dark!

READY . . .

2 tablespoons of olive oil
1 large clove of garlic
a pinch of dried chilli flakes
200g of chestnut mushrooms
sea salt and black pepper
a large handful of flat leaf parsley
3–4 slices of toast

. . . .

a chopping board & sharp knife
a medium-sized frying pan
kitchen paper

STEADY . . .

- Get all your ingredients ready.
- Peel and finely chop the garlic.
- Clean the mushrooms by wiping them with some damp kitchen paper.
- Take a small slice off the bottom of each and either slice them or tear them into chunks.
- Chop the parsley as finely as you can.

GO!

1. Warm the oil in the frying pan and add the garlic and chilli flakes. Warm through for a few minutes to release the flavours.
2. Add the mushrooms and cook them slowly for about 15 minutes, stirring every now and then.
3. Season with sea salt and black pepper.
4. Add the parsley and mix through.
5. Pile them onto the toast and get stuck in. You may or may not want to butter the toast. Try one with butter and one without!

Psst!

- Also gorgeous eaten with Flatbreads (p. 11).

CHINEASY PEASY CHICKEN AND SWEETCORN SOUP

This is always everyone's favourite at the Chinese restaurant. It's so *Easy Peasy* to make at home!

READY . . .

750ml of chicken stock
1 tin of sweetcorn, drained
1 teaspoon of sesame oil
1 teaspoon of sugar
1 free-range chicken breast, cooked
   (see p. 45 or bought ready cooked)
2 teaspoons of cornflour
2 spring onions
1 egg white
1 teaspoon of soy sauce
sea salt

• • • •

a chopping board & sharp knife
a medium-sized saucepan with a lid
a small bowl

STEADY . . .

- Get all your ingredients ready.
- Slice the chicken breast into strips.
- Mix the cornflour with 2 teaspoons of cold water in the small bowl to make a paste.
- Separate the white from the yolk⊙ and lightly beat the egg white with a fork.⊙
- Finely chop the spring onions.⊙

GO!

1. Warm the chicken stock in the pan and add the sliced chicken.
2. Simmer⊙ for 10 minutes.
3. Add the sweetcorn, sesame oil and sugar.
4. While the stock is simmering, drizzle the cornflour paste into the soup, stirring all the time. This thickens the soup and if you don't stir it may go lumpy! Keep going for a few minutes.
5. Add the chopped spring onions.
6. Carefully drizzle the beaten egg white into the soup in a steady stream to make egg ribbons.
7. Serve in small bowls with some soy sauce drizzled on top.

FOR MASH JUST SMASH

Can you believe spuds have been around for more than 7,000 years? They were brought to this country by Sir Walter Raleigh in 1584. There is nothing nicer to eat or easier to make than a pile of steaming, creamy mashed potatoes. You need to use what are called a floury variety, like baking potatoes or Maris Piper.

READY . . .

4–5 large potatoes
sea salt
3–4 tablespoons of milk
a big blob of butter

· · · ·

a chopping board & sharp knife
a potato peeler
a medium-sized saucepan with a lid
a colander
a potato masher

STEADY . . .

- Get all your ingredients ready.
- Peel the potatoes and wash them in cold water.
- Chop them into medium-sized pieces, any old how.

GO!

1. Put the potatoes into the saucepan, add a teaspoon of salt and cover them with cold water. Bring them to the boil. Lower the heat, put the lid on and simmer⊙ for 10–15 minutes.

2. To test if they're cooked, carefully put a sharp knife into one – if it goes in easily, they're cooked. If not, simmer for a further 5 minutes.
3. Drain the potatoes in the colander in the sink, then tip them back into the saucepan and add the milk and butter.
4. Use the masher to smash them until they're smooth, light and fluffy.
5. Put back on the heat for a few minutes to warm them through.

Psst!

- Mix 3–4 tablespoons of grated cheese into the mash, spoon it into an ovenproof dish and sprinkle with some breadcrumbs (see Crumbs, p. 64) and some extra blobs of butter. Bake in the oven (preheat to 180°C/Gas mark 4) for 15 minutes. Very tasty!
- You can use 2 tablespoons of olive oil instead of butter and milk to make a dairy-free mash.

TOMATOES À LA ERIC

Pru's dad was called Eric and there was only one thing he could cook – tomatoes on toast – which the family looked forward to every Sunday morning for breakfast. For the rest of the week he couldn't even find the kitchen! So here's to Eric and his tomatoes! This *Easy Peasy* recipe serves one – just multiply the ingredients if you have friends over to eat!

READY . . .

a large blob of butter
4 large, ripe tomatoes
1 teaspoon of sugar
sea salt and black pepper
2 slices of bread

• • • •

a chopping board & sharp knife
a medium-sized frying pan
a toaster

STEADY . . .

- Get all your ingredients ready.
- Wash and chop the tomatoes any way you want.

GO!

1. Melt the butter in the frying pan on a medium heat.
2. When it begins to sizzle, add the tomatoes and give them a good stir around in the butter.
3. After about 5 minutes add the sugar, a few grindings of black pepper and a good pinch of sea salt. Mix thoroughly.

4. Let the tomatoes cook for about another 10 minutes, stirring regularly. Taste them and add more sea salt if you want. Tomatoes need salt to help bring out their flavour.

5. Pop the bread in the toaster, and when the tomatoes are soft, thick, slushy and sweet, pile them onto the toast and dig in.

Psst!

- If you want to make this a bit more substantial, try breaking an egg or two into the tomatoes after they've been cooking for about 10 minutes. Continue cooking until the eggs are set as you like them. Remember to add a little sea salt and black pepper to the eggs.

- Some people hate tomato skins. If that's you, pick them out, carefully, with a spoon while they're cooking.

SQUASH IT!

At Hallowe'en when you make your witches' lanterns don't throw out the flesh from the pumpkin – cook it!

READY . . .

200g of ready-cubed pumpkin or squash

2–3 tablespoons of olive oil, and some more for drizzling

2 tablespoons of fresh herbs – rosemary, thyme or basil

1 teaspoon of sea salt and black pepper

50g of grated hard, tasty cheese – maybe cheddar or Emmental

2 tablespoons of breadcrumbs

. . . .

a chopping board & sharp knife
a grater or food processor
a non-stick or lined baking tray
a large bowl

STEADY . . .

- Turn on the oven to 200°C/ Gas mark 6.
- Get all your ingredients ready.
- Chop the herbs.
- Make the breadcrumbs – see Crumbs (p. 64).

GO!

1. Put the squash into the bowl and add the oil, fresh herbs, sea salt and plenty of black pepper.
2. Mix everything together and tip onto the baking tray. Bake for about 25 minutes until it's all soft and gooey.
3. Carefully take it out of the oven and cover with the grated cheese and breadcrumbs.
4. Put it back into the oven for another 10 minutes, or until the cheese is yummy and melted and the breadcrumbs are browned and crisp.

Psst!

- If you've used a whole pumpkin, collect the seeds and lay them on a non-stick baking tray. Don't worry about the stray strands of pumpkin – they'll fall off. Sprinkle with sea salt and bake in the oven for about 10–15 minutes. Let them go cold, crack them open and nibble – salted pumpkin seeds for nothing!

CHICKEN NUGGETS

Everybody loves chicken nuggets! It's very quick to make your own – much faster than the delivery man! Why did the chicken get kicked out of school? Because of his fowl language!

READY . . .

3–4 tablespoons of plain flour
sea salt and black pepper
3 free-range, skinned chicken breasts
2 free-range eggs
100g of breadcrumbs
5–6 tablespoons of vegetable oil

. . . .

a chopping board & sharp knife
a small bowl
a plastic bag
2 medium-sized plates
a non-stick or lined baking tray
tongs

STEADY . . .

- Turn on the oven to 190°C/Gas mark 5.
- Get all your ingredients ready.
- Cut the chicken breasts into chunks – these are the nuggets! Remember to wash your hands afterwards!
  - Break the eggs into the bowl,° whisk them and season well with sea salt and black pepper.
  - Make the breadcrumbs – see Crumbs (p. 64) – and spread on a flat plate.

62

GO!

1. Put the flour into the plastic bag with a small teaspoon of salt and some grindings of black pepper.
2. Put the chicken nuggets into the bag and give it a good old shake until they're coated with flour.
3. One by one, dip the nuggets into the egg and then into the breadcrumbs. Make sure they are well coated.
4. Lay them on a plate, cover and pop them in the fridge to firm up for about 20 minutes.
5. Put the chicken nuggets on the baking tray, drizzle with oil and cook in the oven for 15 minutes.
6. Carefully take out the tray, put it on a safe surface and turn each of the nuggets over using tongs. Put them back in the oven and cook for a further 15 minutes or so until the nuggets are sizzling and crispy.
7. Check one to make sure there is no pink in the middle. If there is, cook for another 5 minutes or so.

Psst!

- You can freeze these after they've been cooked. When they're cold, put them in the freezer in a freezer bag. Cook them from frozen at 200°C/Gas mark 6 for 25 minutes.
- You can make these with turkey or any white fish fillets.

CRUMBS

READY...
bread – any kind, old or young,
brown or white

• • • •

a food processor

STEADY...& GO!
1. Tear the bread into the food
   processor, breaking any crusts into
   small pieces, and whizz it until it
   looks like crumbs. Store them in a
   plastic bag in the freezer until you
   need them. You can use them
   frozen too. Just take out however
   much you need when you need it.

Psst!
● If you want toasted breadcrumbs,
  turn on the oven to 200°C/Gas
  mark 6 and toast them on a baking
  tray for about 5 minutes. Don't
  forget them, as they burn very
  quickly!

EGGY POTS

What happened when the elephant crossed the road?
It stood on the chicken!

READY . . .

200g of grated cheddar or Gruyère
   cheese
4 large free-range eggs
sea salt and black pepper
a blob of soft butter

. . . .

a chopping board & sharp knife
a shallow ovenproof dish or 4
   individual ramekins
a baking tray

STEADY . . .

- Turn on the oven to 180°C/Gas
  mark 4
- Get all your ingredients ready.
- Use your fingers and butter the
  insides of the ramekins or dish.

GO!

1. Put half the cheese into the
   ovenproof dish, or share evenly
   between the ramekins. If using
   ramekins, place them on the
   baking tray.
2. Break the eggs on top of the
   cheese, or one egg in each
   ramekin.
3. Season with a little sea salt and
   black pepper.
4. Sprinkle the rest of the cheese over
   the eggs.
5. Dot some pieces of butter on top of
   the cheese and carefully put into
   the oven.
6. Bake for 15 minutes until the eggs
   are cooked and the cheese is all
   gooey and melted.
7. Eat with buttered toast.

Sweetness & Light

BERRY BLUE SOYA SMOOTHIE

So blue, so smooth, so soya!
If you're into purple or blue, then this one's for you.
Blackberries have bits, but you can spit.
Or leave 'em out to smooth it out.

READY . . .

a large handful of blackberries (you
    can use frozen ones, if you want)
a large handful of blueberries
half a banana
200ml of soya milk, or any milk you
    fancy
runny honey, if you like it

. . . .

a blender

STEADY . . . & GO!

1. Put everything into the blender –
   make sure the lid is securely on.
   Then whizz until it's smooth.

Psst!

- If you don't like the bits that
  blackberries leave when they're
  whizzed, just use double the
  amount of blueberries.

MAPLE SYRUP PANCAKES

There are certain times of the week or year that call for a pancake – Saturday mornings, Shrove Tuesday – but they're just as good at any other time. Everyone has a favourite: lemon and sugar, butter and jam, jam and cream or even grilled bacon and tomato. For a real treat, drizzle them with maple syrup.

Maple syrup is a natural sugar collected in the late autumn and early spring from the bark of maple trees in North America and Canada.

READY . . .

100g of plain flour
300ml of semi-skimmed milk
2 large free-range eggs
2 tablespoons of caster sugar
a blob of butter
maple syrup to drizzle on top

. . . .

a food processor
a non-stick frying pan
a spatula
a warm serving plate

STEADY . . .

- Get all your ingredients ready.

GO!

1. Put everything except the butter into the food processor and whizz until you get a smooth batter – thick like custard.
2. Put the frying pan on the stove on a medium heat and add a small blob of butter. When it starts to sizzle, add a tablespoon of the pancake batter.
3. Move the pan from side to side so the batter coats the bottom of the frying pan.
4. Lower the heat and when you see small bubbles all over the surface of the pancake one side is cooked. Use the spatula to carefully turn the pancake over and cook for another 2–3 minutes.
5. Slide it onto a warm plate.
6. Cook all the batter the same way.
7. Drizzle with maple syrup.

CRUNCHY, NUTTY, SWEET AND SALTY

What did the almond say to the dog?
Nothing, almonds can't talk!

Nuts are *soooo* good for you. And if you think there's something weird about the idea of nuts and salt and sugar and *spices*, think again. The only problem with this snack is you might not want to stop eating it – any time of the day or night, in the bath or on the bus! Honestly, once you get going . . . Go on, go nuts.

READY . . .
200g of flaked almonds
a pinch of sea salt
60g of caster or soft brown sugar
2 teaspoons of ground cinnamon
¼ teaspoon of ground cloves
½ teaspoon of ground coriander
1 free-range egg white
Soft butter, for greasing the tray

. . . .

2 mixing bowls
a whisk or electric hand beater
weighing scales
a non-stick or lined baking tray

STEADY . . .
- Turn on the oven to 170°C/Gas mark 3.
- Get all your ingredients ready.
- Separate the egg white from the yolk.☺
- Using *clean* fingers spread some soft butter onto the baking tray.

GO!
1. In one of the mixing bowls, add the almonds, salt, sugar and spices. Mix thoroughly.
2. Beat the egg white until it's soft and stiff.☺
3. Add the almond mixture and mix together very thoroughly and very gently so you keep the air in the egg white.
4. Tip the mixture onto the buttered baking tray and spread it all out into as good a single layer as you can manage.
5. Put it into the oven for 15 minutes, take it out and then give it a good mix. Spread it out again and cook for another 15–20 minutes until the nuts are golden brown.
6. Take out the tray from the oven and let the mixture go cold. Then break it up a bit with your fingers and store in an airtight container.

Psst!

- This is gorgeous as a snack on its own, sprinkled over ice cream or any of the fruit recipes in this book.
- You could also do it with peanuts. If you use salted peanuts, leave out the salt in the ingredients list.

JUST COOKIES

These irresistible cookies are really easy to make and even better to eat. One of life's great pleasures is a warm mug of chai latte and a couple or three *cookies*. It is always better to bake your own treats: that way you know exactly what's in them. Bought cookies usually have a lot of extra *gubbins* in them, which are best avoided.

READY . . .

125g of soft butter
150g of soft brown sugar
1 large free-range egg
100g of plain flour
50g of cocoa powder
½ teaspoon of bicarbonate of soda
3 tablespoons of the filling of your
    choice: peanuts, raisins, chocolate
    chips

. . . .

a large bowl
weighing scales
a wooden spoon or hand-held blender
a sieve
2 large, non-stick or lined baking trays
a cooling rack

STEADY . . .

- Get all your ingredients ready.
- Grease the baking trays with some extra butter.
- Tip the butter and sugar into the bowl and beat with a wooden spoon or hand-held blender until you get a soft, creamy mixture.
- Add the egg and mix everything together.
- Sieve the flour, cocoa powder and bicarbonate of soda into the bowl. Add your tablespoons of fillings and beat again until you get a sticky dough.
- Pop the bowl into the fridge for half an hour or so to allow the dough to firm up.

GO!

1. When you are ready to bake the cookies, turn on the oven to 190°C/Gas mark 5.
2. Take about a half teaspoon of the mixture and roll it into a little ball. Put onto the baking trays, spaced well apart as they'll spread to about three times their size. You'll make about 20–30 cookies, depending on their size.
3. Place each tray into the oven and bake for 8 minutes. Remove from the oven, and after 5 minutes or so lift them carefully onto a wire rack and leave to cool. They'll go nice and crispy.

Psst!

- Once they're cold you can store them in an airtight container and they'll last up to three weeks. (No chance!!!)

73

CHAI LATTE

Chai is an Indian spicy, milky tea which makes a delicious, warming drink. The word *chai* is Hebrew and means 'giving life'. It's a great drink to have any time – after school or with your breakfast. This makes enough for 2–3 mugs.

READY...

2–3 whole cardamom pods
3 mugs of water
1 teabag, any kind
a small chunk of cinnamon stick
a slice of fresh ginger, or a pinch of
    ground ginger
1 teaspoon of soft brown sugar
1 mug of milk, any kind you like –
    cow's, goat's, soya, coconut

● ● ● ●

a small saucepan
a tea strainer
a jug

STEADY...

● Get all your ingredients ready.
● Crush the cardamom pods with
  the back of a spoon or a rolling pin.

GO...

1. Put everything except the milk into
   the saucepan and warm the
   mixture slowly for 20 minutes or
   so to allow the flavours to develop.
2. Carefully pour the tea through the
   strainer into the jug and throw out
   the spices.
3. Add the milk and heat it all up
   again in the saucepan.
4. Taste your chai latte and add more
   sugar if you want it sweeter.

Psst!

● Once it's cold you can keep this in
  the fridge and drink it cold or
  warm it up later.

SO SOYA SMOOTHIE

This banana and oat smoothie makes enough for one big drink. Smoothies are an anytime kind of thing because homemade ones are generally packed with fabulously fresh and good-for-you stuff. They make great breakfasts and really filling, power-packed snacks, especially if they have oats in them, like this one!

READY . . .

1 banana
100ml of plain soya yoghurt
100ml of soya milk – or any other milk you fancy
2 tablespoons of oats
1 tablespoon of runny honey

. . . .

weighing scales or a cup
a blender

STEADY . . . & GO!

1. Put everything into the blender – make sure the lid is securely on – and whizz until it's smooth.

Psst!

- Top tip for runny honey users: dip the tablespoon into a mug of boiling water first. Your honey will just run off the spoon. *Easy Peasy!*

PINK DRINK

Full of fabulous flavours and feisty vitamins!

READY ...

the juice of four oranges, or 200ml of
   fresh orange juice
a large handful of strawberries
a large handful of raspberries
a small handful of ice cubes

. . . .

a chopping board & sharp knife
a liquidiser or blender

STEADY ...

1. Get all your ingredients ready.
2. Cut the oranges in half and
   squeeze the juice.⊙
3. Take the green stems off the top of
   the strawberries – this is known as
   hulling.
4. Rinse the berries in a colander
   under cold water.

GO!

- Put all the ingredients into the
  liquidiser. Put the lid on and whizz
  until smooth.

TAKE TWO - ORANGE ICE CREAM

Take One is ice cream as we know it. *Take Two* is another version, another way. And two ways are always better than one, yes? So, before we start:

What's the best way to stuff a chicken?
Take her out for ice cream!

READY ...
250g of Mascarpone (soft Italian cream cheese)
175g of caster sugar
the juice of 2 oranges, or 100ml fresh orange juice

. . . .

a large bowl
a whisk, or electric hand beater
a tub with a lid for the freezer

STEADY ... & GO!
1. Get all your ingredients ready.
2. Put everything into the bowl and, using the electric hand beater or whisk, beat until smooth.
3. Taste the mixture and add more sugar or more orange if you think it needs it.
4. Pour the ice cream into the tub, put the lid on and put it into the freezer. It'll take a few hours to freeze properly.

Psst!
- You might like to freeze this in individual ramekins, but remember to cover each one with cling film before freezing.
- Try these two other versions of homemade ice cream using 500g of mascarpone, 110g of caster sugar, 200ml of elderflower cordial and a good squeeze of lemon juice; or 250g of mascarpone, 6 tablespoons of ginger syrup from a jar and a good squeeze of lemon juice. Once you've tried these, make up some recipes of your own.
- It keeps for months in the freezer.

Scrumptious
Salads

PERFECT PEPPERS

You can use red, orange or yellow peppers. If you leave peppers out of the fridge for a day, they'll ripen and sweeten and taste even nicer.

READY ...

3 tablespoons of olive oil
4 peppers – any colours
2 large cloves of garlic
a blob of butter
sea salt
a large bunch of fresh basil leaves

• • • •

a chopping board & sharp knife
a medium-sized saucepan with a lid

STEADY ...

- Get all your ingredients ready.
- Prepare the peppers and cut them into strips.☺
- Peel and crush the garlic.☺

GO!

1. Heat the olive oil in the saucepan over a medium heat.
2. Add the peppers and garlic. Mix them carefully but well in the oil, put on the lid, lower the heat and let them cook for about 25 minutes or until they're soft, stirring them occasionally.
3. When they're ready, add some sea salt and the blob of butter.
4. Finish off with a good handful of torn basil leaves.

Psst!

- This is a scrummy sauce either on its own, with some crusty bread and black olives, or delicious with pasta!
- It freezes perfectly.

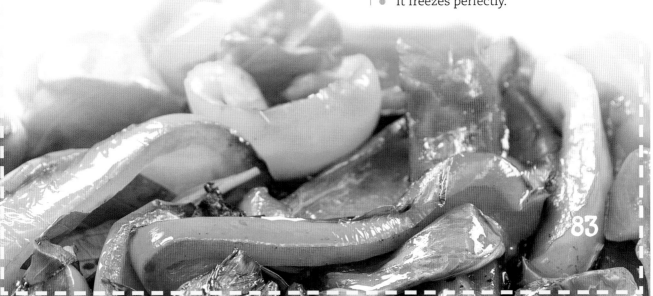

MOORISH CARROT SALAD

We know what you're all asking: Do carrots help you see in the dark? Well, no one can see in the dark because if there's no light, there's no sight. But carrots do contain vitamin A, which improves your vision. The question we're asking is: Why is a carrot orange and pointy? Because if it was round and green it'd be a pea! Carrots make a perfect salad – they are crunchy and full of nutrients. You'll need to make this in advance because it needs time to develop its special flavour – anywhere between two hours and two days will do the trick!

READY . . .
2 cloves of garlic
250g of carrots
a small bunch of parsley
2 tablespoons of olive oil
2 tablespoons of fresh lemon juice
½ teaspoon of ground cumin
½ teaspoon of sweet paprika
a pinch of sea salt
¼ teaspoon of harissa (chilli paste) or
      ¼ teaspoon of cayenne pepper

. . . .

a chopping board & sharp knife
a potato peeler
a bowl
a grater or food processor

STEADY . . .
- Get all your ingredients ready.
- Peel the garlic and chop finely.☺
- Peel and grate the carrots.☺
- Chop the parsley.

GO!

1. Add everything into the bowl and mix thoroughly.
2. Cover with cling film and leave in the fridge until you want to eat it.
3. Mix it up again, taste it and add more sea salt or lemon juice if you think it needs it.
4. Serve either chilled or at room temperature.

Psst!

- If you want to make this Turkish rather than Moroccan, use 60g of natural yoghurt instead of the lemon juice.
- It's lovely with Flatbreads (p. 11) or Koftas (p. 102).
- You could even sprinkle a handful of toasted flaked almonds or sunflower seeds° into the mix.

85

FETA COMPLEE!

Feta is a sheep's milk cheese that has been made in Greece since ancient times. It's a simple curd cheese preserved by bathing it in brine (salty water). It has a salty, tangy taste and adds a big boost of flavour to tomatoes.

READY . . .

6–8 large tomatoes, or a pile of cherry tomatoes
1 small red onion
a large handful of flat leaf parsley
a handful of black olives (Greek Kalamata, if possible) – more, if you want
black pepper
3–4 tablespoons of olive oil
the juice of half a lemon
100–200g of feta cheese

. . . .

a chopping board & sharp knife
a large bowl

STEADY . . .

- Get all your ingredients ready.
- Cut the tomatoes into big chunks, or halve the cherry tomatoes.
- Peel and thinly slice the onion.☺

GO!

1. Put the tomatoes, onion, parsley and olives into the bowl and add a few grindings of black pepper.
2. Drizzle the oil and lemon juice over the salad and mix it all together.
3. Using your hands, break up the feta and sprinkle it over the salad. Use as much or as little as you want, but start with 100g.

Psst!

- The feta is salty, so you probably won't need any other seasoning, but still taste and check!
- It is nice as well with a big handful of spicy rocket leaves.

87

COOL AS A CUCUMBER

You might call this a 'user friendly' kind of salad. It's really easy and it goes brilliantly with so many things.

READY . . .
1 medium-sized cucumber
1 teaspoon of sea salt
1 tablespoon of caster sugar
1 tablespoon of white wine vinegar
a few fronds of fresh dill

• • • •

a chopping board & sharp knife
a vegetable peeler
a colander
a medium-sized bowl

STEADY . . .
- Get all your ingredients ready.
- Peel the cucumber, slice it lengthways as thinly as you can and leave it to drain in the colander over the sink for 10 minutes.
- Finely chop the dill.

GO!
1. Put everything, except the dill, into the bowl. Mix it together really well, leave for about an hour to let the flavours develop. This is called macerating.
2. Put the salad into a serving dish and sprinkle with the dill. Cover it and put it into the fridge to chill a bit before eating.

Psst!
- Try it with Brain Food (p. 119), or it's very nice in a baked potato with a blob of sour cream.
- If you want very, very thin slices of cucumber, use the slicing blade on a food processor.

HAIL CAESAR SALAD!

This salad was invented in the 1920s by an Italian-American chef called Caesar Cardini. It's highly unlikely his namesake, Julius Caesar (100–44BC), ever tasted it! He didn't know what he was missing. This is an *Easy Peasy* version.

READY ...

1 cos lettuce, or 2 little gem lettuces
4 handfuls of croutons (see p. 91)
2 roasted chicken breasts (see p. 45)
3–4 tablespoons of grated Parmesan

For the dressing ...

4 tablespoons sour cream
1 tablespoon lemon juice
1 teaspoon Dijon mustard
sea salt and black pepper

• • • •

a chopping board & sharp knife
a large salad bowl
a grater or food processor
a small bowl

STEADY ...

- Get all your ingredients ready.
- Wash, drain and dry the lettuce.
- Cut or tear the chicken into bite-size pieces.

GO!

1. In a small bowl, mix together the sour cream, lemon juice and mustard. Add a little sea salt and black pepper and whisk it all together.
2. Put the lettuce, croutons and chicken into the large bowl.
3. Pour on the dressing and mix it all up.
4. Add the Parmesan.

Psst!

- This is best eaten freshly made.
- To make your own sour cream, add 2 teaspoons of lemon juice to a small carton of double cream and leave for half an hour.
- If you're after a real surprise, try adding 3–4 chopped-up anchovies into the dressing. It adds a whole other wonderfulness!

CROUTONS

These 'bread cubes' are perfect for salads, soups and snacks, and there are lots of variations.

READY ...

bread – any kind, brown or white, young or old
3–4 tablespoons of olive oil

. . . .

a chopping board & sharp knife
a medium-sized bowl
a non-stick or lined baking tray

STEADY ... & GO!

1. Turn on the oven to 200°C/Gas mark 6.
2. Get all your ingredients ready.
3. Either cut the bread into small cubes or tear it into small pieces.
4. Put them into the bowl, add the olive oil and mix it all well together.
5. Tip them onto the baking tray and bake for about 10 minutes until they're brown and crisp. Do check them after about 6 minutes because they can burn very quickly.

Psst!

- These freeze brilliantly. To keep them crisp, just pop them into a hot oven (200°C/Gas mark 6) for 5 minutes.
- Use with Beautiful Pea Green Boat (p. 30) and Hail Caesar Salad (p. 90).
- Try adding some crushed garlic and Parmesan before putting them into the oven, or maybe black pepper and oregano for a different taste.

Divine Dinners

KNOCK-UP TART

A tart is a wonderful thing. It's like a one-pot wonder with just about everything you need for a gorgeous and good-for-you meal all sitting on the same crisp, crumbly, melt-in-the-mouth pastry base.

READY...

1 red and 1 yellow pepper
1 small red onion
150g of chorizo sausage
100g of grated strong cheddar cheese
20g of flat leaf parsley
sea salt and black pepper
375g of ready-rolled shortcrust pastry
5 tablespoons of tomato puree

· · · ·

a chopping board & sharp knife
weighing scales
a grater or food processor
a medium bowl
a non-stick or lined baking tray

STEADY...

- Turn on the oven to 180°C/Gas mark 4.
- Get all your ingredients ready.
- De-seed the peppers and slice thinly.☺
- Peel and slice the onion as thinly as you can.☺
- Chop the parsley.
- Cut the chorizo into small chunks.

GO!

1. Put everything, except the tomato puree and the pastry, into the bowl and sprinkle with sea salt and black pepper. Mix it all together.
2. Lay your pastry on the baking tray and turn up the edges to make a lip. This keeps the filling in.
3. Spread the base of the pastry, up to the lip, with the tomato puree.
4. Tip everything in the bowl into the pastry case, spread it around evenly and place it in the oven for about 20–25 minutes. Check it after 20 minutes. It's ready when it's bubbling and looking golden brown.

Psst!

- This is heavenly eaten hot with a crisp, green salad, or cold as a lunchbox treat.
- You can leave out the chorizo, if you like.

TUTTI FRUTTI CHICKEN CURRY

When we started thinking about this recipe, we tried to find some good curry jokes. You see, you've got to laugh when you eat curry otherwise you'll cry – with the heat of the chilli! Then we thought, we can't spend our days telling jokes, we've got to cook. So we created Tutti Frutti Chicken Curry. This isn't hot; it's mild and sweet and pleasing.

READY . . .

3 tablespoons of vegetable oil
1 large onion
2 cloves of garlic
1½–2 tablespoons of medium curry powder
1 tablespoon of tomato puree
400g of free-range chicken breasts
1 tin of chopped tomatoes
½ of the same tin of water
a handful of sultanas, or more, depending on how sweet you like things
sea salt and black pepper

. . . .

a chopping board & sharp knife
a medium-sized casserole dish or saucepan with a lid

STEADY . . .

- Get all your ingredients ready.
- Peel and slice the onion☺ and chop the garlic☺ as finely as you can.
- Cut the chicken into chunks. Remember to wash your hands afterwards!

GO!

1. Heat the oil in the casserole dish. When it's hot, add the onions and garlic and cook, stirring often, until they start to look soft and golden.
2. Add the curry powder and tomato puree and cook all together for a couple of minutes.
3. Add the chicken, stirring it around in the spicy onions until it's well coated. Let it cook for a few minutes, but keep stirring.

4. Add the tomatoes, water and sultanas, and a good pinch of sea salt and black pepper, then turn up the heat so everything starts to bubble.

5. Lower the heat, put the lid on and simmer⊙ gently for 30–40 minutes. It's ready when the sauce has gone all thick and scrummy.

6. Taste it and add more sea salt and black pepper, if you think it needs it. You decide. Trust your tastebuds!

Psst!

● To add even more flavour, chop up some fresh coriander and sprinkle it over the chicken just before you serve it.

● This is good with boiled rice,⊙ Flatbreads (p. 11) and mango chutney.

● It'll keep in the fridge, in an airtight container, for two days. It's delicious cold!

● You can freeze it, too!

SPANISH OMELETTE

What do you call a really good omelette?
Eggcellent!

We all love omelettes of all kinds – Spanish, Italian, British. They're especially good with hot, crusty bread and a salad. So, let's get cracking!

READY . . .

5 large free-range eggs
sea salt and black pepper
3 tablespoons of grated cheddar or
   Parmesan
2 tablespoons of olive oil
2 medium onions
6 new potatoes

. . . .

a chopping board & sharp knife
a small saucepan with a lid
a colander
a grill
a medium ovenproof, non-stick frying
   pan
a medium bowl
a grater or food processor
a whisk or a fork

STEADY . . .

- Get all your ingredients ready.
- Wash the potatoes, put them in the saucepan with a teaspoon of salt and cover with cold water. Put the lid on and bring them to a boil over a high heat. Lower the heat and simmer☺ for about 10 minutes until they're nearly cooked.☺
- Drain them in the colander and let them cool.
- Peel and slice the onions as finely as you can.☺
- Grate the cheese.
- Break the eggs into a bowl☺ and add a teaspoon of sea salt, a few grindings of black pepper and the grated cheese. Whisk it all up together with a fork or small hand whisk.

96

GO!

1. Heat the oil in the frying pan. When it's hot, add the onions. Turn them over now and then, and cook until soft and brown at the edges – about 10–15 minutes.
2. Cut the potatoes into small cubes or slices, removing the skins that fall off. Add them to the onions. Turn them over carefully, so they don't break, and cook for a few minutes.
3. Turn the grill to high.
4. Pour the egg mixture over the potatoes and onions and let it cook slowly for about 10 minutes until it's got a crusty bottom!
5. Now pop the frying pan under the grill for a few minutes until the eggs look firm and golden brown.

Psst!

- Try adding three handfuls of fresh spinach to the potato and onion mix. Turn it all over gently until the spinach wilts, then pour over the eggs.
- This is wonderful eaten hot or cold, and is great for picnics or in lunchboxes.

IT'S A BIT CHILLI!

A real Wild West recipe! Good to eat in a bowl in front of the fire on a cold winter's evening. Get warmed up inside and out!

READY . . .

2 tablespoons of vegetable oil
1 teaspoon of chilli powder or chilli flakes
1 teaspoon of ground cumin
¼ teaspoon of ground cinnamon
1 large onion
2 large cloves of garlic
1 red pepper
500g of lean minced beef
1 tin of chopped tomatoes
1 tin of kidney beans
½ teaspoon of sea salt

• • • •

a chopping board & sharp knife
a large ovenproof dish or saucepan with a lid
a colander

STEADY . . .

- Turn on the oven to 180°C/Gas mark 4.
- Get all your ingredients ready.
- Peel and chop the onion☺ and garlic.☺
- De-seed and chop the pepper.☺
- Drain the beans in the colander and rinse under cold water.

GO!

1. Warm the oil in the ovenproof dish/saucepan on a medium heat.
2. Add the spices and stir them around for a minute or two.
3. Add the onions, garlic and pepper. Stir them around, then lower the heat, put the lid on and let them soften for 10 minutes. Check them once or twice, giving them a stir.
4. Turn the heat to high and add the mince. Mix it in, breaking up the clumps until it's all browned.
5. Add the tomatoes, kidney beans and a large pinch of sea salt. Mix thoroughly and let it come to a simmer.☺
6. Put the lid on and place in the oven for 40 minutes.
7. Taste it and check there's enough salt.

Psst!

- This is lovely eaten with Flatbreads (p. 11) or popped into a wrap or bun and served with a dollop of natural yoghurt or Adorable Avocado (p. 25).
- Try some freshly chopped coriander sprinkled over the top just before you serve it. Really good!
- For a vegetarian option, you can use soya mince instead with a teaspoon of paprika.

LEMON CHICKEN AND POTATO WEDGES

If you're a meat eater like us, then you can't do better than eat chicken. It's full of good things like protein, vitamins and minerals, and very low in fat. That said, we just want you to learn to cook with love and enjoy everything you make. So, get cracking with this guaranteed crowd pleaser!

READY . . .

4–6 boneless free-range chicken
   thighs, depending on how big they
   are
1 large red onion
6 cloves of garlic

4 baking potatoes
1 large lemon
sea salt and black pepper
3 teaspoons of runny honey
2 tablespoons of olive oil
a small handful of fresh thyme
4 sprigs of fresh rosemary

• • • •

a chopping board & sharp knife
a large ovenproof roasting tin or dish
a small bowl

STEADY . . .

- Turn on the oven 200°C/
  Gas mark 6.
- Get all your ingredients ready.
- Peel the onion and slice it thickly.○
- Peel the garlic cloves○ but leave
  them whole.
- Scrub the potatoes in their skins
  and slice them lengthways into
  wedges.
- Cut the lemon in half and slice one
  of the halves thinly.

100

GO!

1. Put the chicken, onion, garlic, potatoes and lemon slices into the ovenproof dish. Season well with sea salt and black pepper.

2. In the small bowl mix together the juice from the half lemon, the honey and the oil, then pour this over the chicken, mixing it all together with your hands so that everything is well-coated in the dressing. Remember to wash your hands afterwards!

3. Add the thyme and rosemary and cook for an hour or until the potatoes are beginning to crisp. Slice the chicken to make sure the meat isn't pink. If it is, put back in the oven for another 5 minutes.

Psst

- Make lemon potatoes the same way – just leave out the chicken!

KOFTAS

What's a kofta, you ask? Well, basically it's a spiced meatball which came from Persia, but is now eaten all over the world. It's thought there are nearly 300 different kinds of kofta in Turkey. Let's start by making just one!

READY ...

500g of minced lamb
2 small red onions
3 cloves of garlic
2 ripe tomatoes
1 teaspoon of chilli flakes
a large handful of flat leaf parsley
a good pinch of sea salt and black
    pepper
vegetable oil for frying

. . . .

a chopping board & sharp knife
a food processor
a large bowl
a pastry brush
a grill

STEADY ...

- Get all your ingredients ready.
- Peel the onions and cut into quarters.☺
- Peel the garlic.☺
- Cut the tomatoes into halves or quarters, depending on their size.
- Put the lamb into the food processor and whizz it a couple of times until it looks like a paste.
- Add all the remaining ingredients – except the oil – and whizz some more until you have a paste.
- Put the mixture into a clean bowl and bring it together with your hands. Cover and leave in the fridge to firm up for about 30 minutes.

GO!

1. Heat the grill to hot – about 200°C.
2. Pull off chunks of mixture and roll into small sausages or oblongs. Lay them on the grill pan and brush each with a little oil.
3. Grill for 4 minutes on each side until cooked and crispy.

Psst!

- These are really good with lots of our recipes. Try them with Adorable Avocado (p. 25), Perfect Peppers (p. 83), Moorish Carrot Salad (p. 84) or Pea, Parsley and Mint Dip (p. 13). Shall we go on?
- You can try lots of different spice mixes as well. Try cumin and coriander seeds or some paprika. You can also add fresh, chopped mint into the mix.
- Serve with lemon wedges.
- If you haven't got a grill, you can fry them in a few tablespoons of sizzling vegetable oil. They'll need about the same cooking time.

RIB TICKLERS

Chinese sweet and sour ribs are sticky and delicious.
Hello there, China!

READY . . .

1 pack of small pork ribs, about 250g
1 onion
1 green pepper
1 teaspoon of sea salt

For the sauce:

a chunk of fresh ginger
2 cloves of garlic
2 tablespoons of vegetable oil
1 tablespoon of brown sugar
2 teaspoons of white wine vinegar
2 tablespoons of soy sauce

. . . .

a chopping board & sharp knife
an ovenproof dish
tin foil
a grater
a small saucepan
a medium-sized bowl
tongs

STEADY . . .

- Get all your ingredients ready.
- De-seed and slice the green pepper and roughly chop the onion.
- Grate the fresh ginger and crush the garlic.

GO!

1. Turn on the oven to 150°C/Gas mark 2.
2. Put the ribs into the ovenproof dish with the onion and pepper. Sprinkle over the salt.
3. Cover with tin foil, put in the oven and cook for 1 hour.
4. Put all the sauce ingredients into the bowl and mix
5. Carefully remove the ribs from the oven. Pour the sauce over them, making sure all are well covered.
6. Increase the oven temperature to 190°C/Gas mark 5, then carefully put the tray back into the oven, covered with foil, and cook for another 30 minutes.
7. Let the ribs cool a bit before diving in.

CHOW-CHOW NOODLES

Once you get the knack of these easy Chinese noodles you can make them in a flash with anything you fancy. Chop, chop!

READY . . .

250g of instant noodles
1 litre of water
1 tablespoon of groundnut or corn oil
1 large clove of garlic
1 slice of smoked bacon
50g of green beans or mangetout
½ a red or green pepper
3 teaspoons of soy sauce
2 teaspoons of rice wine
a pinch of sugar
1 free-range chicken breast, cooked
   (see p. 45)
4 spring onions
1 teaspoon of sesame oil

• • • •

a chopping board & sharp knife
a medium-sized saucepan
a colander
a wok, or wide frying pan

STEADY . . .

- Get all your ingredients ready.
- Chop the garlic[☉] and spring onions,[☉] slice the peppers as finely as you can,[☉] cut the beans in half if they're very long.
- Chop the bacon into small pieces.
- Slice the cooked chicken.

GO!

1. Put the water in the saucepan and bring to a boil. Add a teaspoon of salt.
2. Carefully add the noodles to the pan of boiling salted water. Stir them around and cook for 4–5 minutes, then drain them in the colander over the sink. This is a hot and heavy job so you may want to ask an adult for help.
3. Heat the oil in the wok or wide frying pan.
4. Add the garlic and let it sizzle a bit to release the flavours.
5. Now add the bacon and let it sizzle and brown, stirring all the time.
6. Add the green beans or mangetout and the pepper, and stir them around too.

7. Next add the soy sauce and rice wine, and after a minute or two add the noodles and mix everything very thoroughly.

8. Add the sugar and the shredded chicken, and a splash of water if the noodles look a bit dry.

9. Stir for a few more minutes and, finally, add the spring onions and sesame oil.

10. Pile into bowls and go for it!

107

YOU'RE A NUT BURGER!

Not so long ago, the idea of a vegetarian burger was like imagining aliens on earth. And a nut burger – well, you'd have had to be nuts to eat that! Today, we all love them. They've become part of our everyday food. They're delicious. Try them!

READY...

1 small red onion
1 large clove of garlic
1 green pepper
1 courgette
50g each of unsalted almonds and
    peanuts
100g of breadcrumbs (see Crumbs,
    p. 64)
1 tablespoon of grated cheddar

1 free-range egg
sea salt and black pepper

• • • •

a chopping board & sharp knife
a food processor
a mixing bowl
a grater
a lightly oiled non-stick baking tray
a spatula

STEADY . . .

- Turn on the oven to 180°C/Gas mark 4.
- Get all your ingredients ready.
- Peel and chop the onion☺ and garlic☺ any old how.
- Wash the pepper and remove the seeds and core, then chop it up.☺
- Wash the courgette, top and tail it,☺ and slice it.

GO!

1. Add all the vegetables and nuts to the food processor and whizz until they look like a paste.
2. Put the mixture into the bowl with the breadcrumbs, cheese, beaten egg, sea salt and black pepper. Mix it all together thoroughly with your hands and pop it in the fridge for 20 minutes to firm up.
3. Now, using your hands, make burger shapes with the mixture and put them onto the baking tray.
4. Cook in the oven for 25 minutes and then, using the spatula, carefully turn them over and cook the other side for another 15 minutes.

Psst!

- These are gorgeous cold, so good for lunchboxes, snacks and picnics.
- For a different taste, you could add a handful of chopped parsley and two teaspoons of mild curry powder or garam masala into the mixture. These are lovely with natural yoghurt too.
- Great with Adorable Avocado (p. 25), Moorish Carrot Salad (p. 84), Pea, Parsley and Mint Dip (p. 13), Perfect Peppers (p. 83) and Soo-go! (p. 114).
- They'll keep in the fridge in an airtight container for up to 3 days.
- They freeze brilliantly too and just need a blast in a hot oven – 200°C/ Gas mark 6 – for 8–10 minutes.

109

GNOCCHI

You'll love learning how to make these potato dumplings. They are a bit messy, but that's part of the fun. Once they are ready to go, they cook in minutes.

READY...

about 450g of floury potatoes (Desiree or Maris Piper)
about 250g of plain flour
1 large free-range egg yolk
100g of butter
2–3 tablespoons of grated cheddar or Parmesan

. . . .

a chopping board & sharp knife
a medium-sized saucepan with a lid
a large bowl
a sieve
a colander
a potato masher
weighing scales
a tray lined with greaseproof paper and dusted with flour
a serving bowl or large dish

STEADY...

- Get all your ingredients ready.
- Separate the egg yolk from the white.☺
- Wash the potatoes and cut them in half. Put them into the saucepan and cover with cold water. *Don't add any salt because it'll make the potatoes watery*. Bring them to the boil and cook them, lid on, for 15–20 minutes. They're ready when a skewer slides in easily. Drain them and allow them to cool. Slip off the skins and mash them until they're smooth.

GO!

1. Weigh the potatoes in a bowl and add the **same weight** of sieved plain flour.
2. Add the egg yolk.
3. Now dip your hands in a little flour and mix everything together thoroughly to make a well blended dough.
4. Cut the dough into 8 pieces and roll each one into a sausage shape.

5. Cut each 'sausage' into 2–3cm pieces and make some ridges on them by pressing the back of a fork into each one. Put them onto the floured tray. Now you're ready to cook them . . .

6. Bring a large saucepan of salted water to the boil, then add the potato dumplings, being very careful not to splash yourself. As soon as they rise to the surface, they're ready – about 3–5 minutes.

7. Drain them well in the colander and tip them into a warm serving dish. Add the butter and cheese!

Psst!

- These are perfect drizzled with Hey, Basil Pesto! (p. 32) or served with lots of Soo-go! (p. 114).
- You can freeze them and cook them straight from frozen.

S'BEANS

Sausages and beans is such a good combo. S'beans are homemade beans at their most delicious. They're a bit of work, but so worth it. Sausage lovers all over the world have a saying: 'If at first you don't succeed, fry, fry and fry again.'

READY . . .

1 tablespoon of olive oil
500g of sausages – any kind will do
100g of unsmoked lardons (bacon bits)
1 red onion
1 large clove of garlic, or 2 small ones
2 tins of cannellini beans
½ teaspoon of chilli flakes
1 teaspoon of sugar
1 tin of chopped tomatoes
200ml of chicken stock
sea salt
a large handful of parsley

. . . .

a chopping board & sharp knife
a colander
a medium-sized casserole dish
   with a lid

STEADY . . .

- Turn on the oven to 200°C/Gas mark 6.
- Get all your ingredients ready.
- Peel and slice the onion☺ and garlic☺ as thinly as you can.
- Drain the cannellini beans and rinse under cold water.
- Chop the parsley and set aside.

GO!

1. Heat the oil in the casserole dish and add the sausages, lardons, onion and garlic. Mix them together, put the lid on and cook in the oven for 20 minutes.
2. While that's happening, mix together the beans, chilli flakes, sugar, tomatoes, stock and two good-sized pinches of sea salt.
3. After 20 minutes, take the sausages out of the oven and turn them over.
4. Add the bean mixture and stir together gently. Put the lid back on and cook in the oven for another 20 minutes before you take off the lid and give everything another good stir.
5. Turn the heat down to 170°C/Gas mark 3 and let it cook for another 30–40 minutes. Check it every now and then, and add a little more stock or water if you think it's getting a bit dry.
6. When it's ready, add the parsley, taste the sauce and add a little more sea salt if you think it needs it.

Psst!

- Beans on toast! If you've eaten all the sausages and have some beans left over, give them a light mash with a fork or a potato masher and pile them onto hot toast. Eat them on their own or with an egg.
- Once cold it'll keep in an airtight container in the fridge for two days.
- The dish also freezes fabulously.

SOO-GO

Fresh tomato sauce in Italy is called *sugo* – pronounced 'soo-go'! It's very quick and *Easy Peasy* to make because it's made there every day. *Mamma mia!*

READY . . .

3 tablespoons of olive oil
1 clove of garlic
1 small onion
1 tin of chopped tomatoes
sea salt
a handful of fresh basil

• • • •

a chopping board & sharp knife
a medium-sized saucepan with a lid

STEADY . . .

- Get all your ingredients ready.
- Peel and chop the onion☺ and garlic.☺

1. Warm the oil in the saucepan over a low heat.
2. Add the garlic and let it cook slowly until you start to smell it – but be careful not to let it burn.
3. Add the onion, turn everything round in the oil and cook slowly with the lid on for about 5–10 minutes until the onions are pale and sweet-smelling.
4. Add the chopped tomatoes, stir again and raise the heat to a simmer,[○] letting the sauce cook for 30–40 minutes. Try balancing the lid of the pot on a wooden spoon so the sauce gently reduces as it cooks.
5. Taste it and add sea salt, a little at a time, till it tastes good.
6. Finish with some torn basil leaves.

Psst!

- Great for using as a pasta sauce or as the base for a pizza.
- This is also the sauce you'll need to go with Gnocchi (p. 110) and Balls (p. 116).
- Perfect for freezing.
- Sometimes tomatoes can be a little sour; if so, add a little sugar.

115

BALLS IN SOO-GO

First make Soo-go! You'll find the recipe on page 114.

READY ...

1 medium onion
a small handful of flat leaf parsley
1 large free-range egg yolk
500g of minced pork
4–5 tablespoons of breadcrumbs
    (see Crumbs, p. 64)
1 tablespoon of grated Parmesan
1 large teaspoon of sea salt and some
    black pepper
3–4 tablespoons of olive oil

• • • •

a chopping board & sharp knife
a grater
a medium-sized bowl
a large frying pan

STEADY ...

- Get all your ingredients ready.
- Peel and chop the onion as finely as you can.☺
- Chop the parsley.
- Separate the egg yolk from the white.☺

GO!

1. Put everything – except the olive oil – into a bowl and mix it all together with your hands. It needs to be really well combined, so squidge and squeeze away!
2. Roll the mixture into small balls, about the size of a golf ball or even a ping-pong ball, whatever you like best. This is easier if you dampen your hands a bit first with some water.
3. When the meatballs are all rolled, heat the oil in the frying pan. When it's hot, put them in a few at a time. Cook them on a medium heat, gently turning them so they cook on all sides and get nice and brown.

4. While they are cooking, pour your Soo-go sauce into a pot and warm it through. Gently lay the meatballs on top, then put the lid on, turn the heat down and allow it all to cook for about 45 minutes. Check it every now and then, and if it's getting dry add a splash of water.

5. Turn the meatballs in the sauce so they cook right through.
6. Check the flavour and add more sea salt or pepper, if needed.

Psst!
- Add a small handful of torn basil leaves to brighten the taste.
- You can make these balls with half minced turkey and half pork, or half pork and half beef.
- This is just lovely served on pasta too – any pasta you fancy. Oh, and lots of crusty bread!
- You can also freeze the whole dish – balls and soo-go!

BRAIN FOOD

One thing we know for sure is that oily fish is good for you. Brain food is what we call it, so if your brain needs waking up, eat some salmon. And do you know the best way to catch a salmon? Get someone to throw it at you!

READY . . .

4 salmon fillets
sea salt and 6–8 black peppercorns
2 bay leaves
1 fish stock cube or gel pot, for extra
    flavour

. . . .

a medium-sized saucepan with a lid
kitchen paper

STEADY . . . & GO!

1. Get all your ingredients ready.
2. Put the fish into the saucepan with a little sea salt and the black peppercorns.
3. Add the bay leaves and stock cube, if you're using one, and *just* cover the salmon with cold water.
4. Put the lid on and slowly bring to the boil over a medium heat. Let the fish cook for about 4 minutes, then turn off the heat. Leave the salmon in the saucepan until it's completely cold. This will take a while.

5. When you're ready to eat, very carefully lift the fillets out of the stock and let them drain on some kitchen paper.

Psst!

- You can leave out the stock cube if you want and just use water, but some salmon fillets need a little flavour boost when they're cooking.
- This is *so* good with Cool as a Cucumber (p.88), with Hey, Basil Pesto! (p. 32) and Hey, Rocket Pesto! (p. 24), or Green Pea Hummus (p. 20) and the Pea, Parsley and Mint Dip (p. 13).
- It's also fab with some plain boiled new potatoes, peas and mayonnaise.

OVER T'OFU!

Tofu is made from soya milk from soya beans and is made much the same way as cheese is made from ordinary milk. It can be savoury or sweet. Tofu came from China about 2,000 years ago – apparently invented by a prince called Liu An. It's an important part of a vegetarian diet as it has loads of protein in it. Today you can buy lots of different kinds, but here's a simple one for you to try. By the way, does anyone have any tofu jokes? We can't think of any!

READY . . .

400g of extra-firm tofu
100ml of soy sauce
1 tablespoon of sugar
1 tablespoon of white wine vinegar
4 burger buns
sliced cheddar cheese, alfalfa sprouts
    or cress, and sliced cucumber or
    radishes to garnish
2 tablespoons of olive oil

. . . .

a chopping board & sharp knife
kitchen paper
a medium-sized dish
a small saucepan
a medium-sized non-stick frying pan

STEADY . . .

- Get all your ingredients ready.
- Drain the tofu and dry well with kitchen paper. Slice it into four pieces and put them into the dish.

GO!

1. Make a marinade by putting the soy sauce, sugar and white wine vinegar into the small saucepan. Cook it on a low heat for about 7 minutes, stirring it a few times.
2. Pour it over the tofu and let it soak up the juices for 15–20 minutes. Turn the pieces over once or twice during this time.
3. Arrange the cheese in the rolls with the sprouts, cucumber, cress or radishes – any or all will do. You're looking for some crunch!
4. Now heat the oil in the frying pan, and when it's hot carefully put the tofu slices in and cook for two minutes on each side.
5. Pile them into the buns and go for it!

MOZZARELLA EGGS

If you're like us, you normally eat mozzarella on a pizza – right? Did you know it is just as nice on its own drizzled with olive oil? Or try it in this *Easy Peasy* omelette.

READY ...

olive oil
5 large free-range eggs
200g of mozzarella
sea salt and black pepper

. . . .

a chopping board
a medium-sized bowl
a fork
a medium-sized non-stick frying pan

STEADY ...

- Get all your ingredients ready.
- Break the eggs⊙ into the bowl. Add some sea salt and pepper and beat them with a fork.
- Drain the liquid from the mozzarella and tear it into thin strips.

GO!

1. Warm a little olive oil in the frying pan and when it starts to sizzle pour in the eggs and let them cook for a few minutes.
2. Place the mozzarella strips on top of the eggs and let them start to melt and fluff up.
3. Just before the egg goes solid, fold the omelette in half and cook for another 2 minutes.

Psst!

- This is extra delicious served with a salad of sliced tomatoes and torn basil leaves. Just give it a dressing of a little sea salt and a drizzle of olive oil.
- Wonderful eaten cold.

Fabulous
Fruits

GRANNY SMITH'S FRUIT

We've never had a granny called Smith. We've never even met one. But this is a recipe for Granny Smith apples – bright green and crisp, you can buy them all year round. So if we're clear about this, let's cook!

READY ...

3 large ripe peaches
3 large ripe plums
1 large Granny Smith apple
30g of walnuts or flaked almonds
100ml of unsweetened orange juice

. . . .

a chopping board & sharp knife
a medium-sized saucepan with a lid
a serving bowl

STEADY ...

- Get all your ingredients ready.
- Take the stones out of the peaches and plums.☺ Chop the flesh up any old how.
- Peel and core the apple.☺ Chop it up any old how.
- Toast the walnuts or flaked almonds,☺ whichever you are using.

GO!

1. Add the fruit, nuts and fruit juice into the saucepan, put the lid on and cook over a low heat for about 10 minutes.
2. Take the lid off and stir the fruits together. Cook for another 10–15 minutes until the fruits are soft – but not too soft, you need to leave a little bite!
3. Tip into a serving bowl.

Psst!

- This is very good on its own – warm or cold – or with yoghurt or cream.
- It'll freeze beautifully, and keep well in the fridge in an airtight container.

RHUBARB AND BANANA FOOL

What do you say to your bananas when you leave for school in the morning? 'I'm going, Bananas!'

Did you know a stick of rhubarb dipped in sugar used to be a popular sweet for children in parts of Britain and Sweden? In fact, it's still eaten like this in lots of places. Rhubarb is sour but not when it snuggles up beside a banana!

READY . . .
about 500g of rhubarb
1 orange
120g of soft light-brown sugar
3–4 ripe bananas

. . . .

a chopping board & sharp knife
weighing scales
a medium-sized saucepan with a lid
a grater
a food processor

STEADY . . .
- Grate the rind of the orange and extract the juice.☺
- Slice the rhubarb into chunks.

GO!
1. Place the rhubarb in the saucepan and add the orange juice, zest and sugar. Put the lid on and cook on a low heat until the fruit is soft – about 10–15 minutes.
2. Take it off the heat and let it cool.
3. Peel the bananas and put them into the food processor with the rhubarb. Whizz a few times. You want it thick and lumpy.
4. Taste it and add some more sugar if you think it needs it.

Psst!
- Try adding a bit of chopped-up stem ginger to give it an extra sparkle.

125

MORE FRUITS...

We like to bang on about fruit because fruit is good. It's good hot and it's good cold. It's good at any time of the day, and it's good for any number of people. So here's some more good fruity ideas!

One
200g of fresh apricots, 2 eating apples, a good splash of unsweetened apple or orange juice

Two
4 large peaches, a punnet of strawberries, a tablespoon of elderflower cordial

Three
4 eating apples, 2 large pears, a handful of sultanas, a splash of ginger cordial and a splash of water

READY ... STEADY ... & GO!
1. Get all your ingredients together.
2. Take the stones out of any of the fruits that have them⊙ and peel and core any apples.⊙
3. Put everything into the saucepan, put on the lid and bring to a simmer on a medium heat. Then lower the heat and leave for about 10 minutes.
4. Continue cooking without the lid until the fruit is soft but not mushy – you still want a little bite.
5. That's it! Can't get much easier than this!

Psst!
- The thing about cooked fruit is it's delicious on its own or with lots of other foods like cereal, muesli, porridge, yoghurt, cream, toasted chopped nuts, chia seeds or indeed any other seed.
- A little cinnamon is fab with apples and pears, as is a handful of sultanas.
- For sheer heaven, crumble some digestive biscuits over the top!

MARVELLOUS MUESLI

Homemade muesli is a marvellous thing. It's bursting with good foods, fabulous flavours and a powerful energy booster. It was invented around 1900 by a Swiss doctor whose patients needed a diet rich in fresh fruits and vegetables. You'll have to leave this one overnight, but believe us, it's worth it.

READY . . .

2 ripe pears
80g of jumbo oats
a handful of sultanas – around 25g
300ml of unsweetened apple juice
a handful of flaked almonds, if you
    want them
3 tablespoons of natural yoghurt
a drizzle of runny honey

. . . .

a chopping board & sharp knife
weighing scales
a medium-sized serving bowl
cling film

STEADY . . .

- Get all your ingredients ready.
- Cut the pears into quarters (no need to peel), take out the cores and chop them into small pieces.☺
- Add them to a bowl with the oats, sultanas and apple juice. The apple juice should just cover the mixture.
- Cover it with cling film and leave in the fridge overnight.
- Toast the flaked almonds☺ and place to one side.

GO!

1. Next morning add 3 tablespoons of natural yoghurt and mix it in.
2. Serve with a drizzle of runny honey and the toasted almonds, if you're using them. You may find the pears are sweet enough without the honey, but the almonds add an extra fab factor.

SCRUMPTIOUS SLAPPLEBERRY

Did you know, more apples are grown and eaten than any other fruit in the world, and strawberries have been around since the Romans? You know tomatoes are really fruits not vegetables? Well, strawberries are not really fruits either, they're members of the rose family!

READY . . .

2 Bramley cooking apples
150–200ml of unsweetened apple juice
1 tablespoon of demerara sugar
1 punnet of strawberries

. . . .

a chopping board & sharp knife
a medium-sized saucepan with a lid
a serving bowl

STEADY . . .

- Get all your ingredients ready.
- Peel and core the apples, and chop them into chunks.☺
- Slice the green stem off the strawberries and cut them in half, if they're very big.

GO!

1. Put the apples into the saucepan with the apple juice and sugar.
2. Put on the lid and cook on a low heat for about 10 minutes until the apples are getting soft.
3. Add the strawberries and mix through very gently so you don't break them.
4. Take the lid off and cook for another 10–15 mins until the strawberries are very soft.
5. Cool and tip into a serving bowl.

Psst!

- This can be eaten warm or cold, but it's nicest cold.
- It's very good with yoghurt or cream, or added to your breakfast cereal.
- Try adding some chia seeds while it's still warm.
- It'll freeze beautifully, or store well in the fridge in an airtight container.

The Knack

Before we even begin this bit we have to tell you something *really* important. *Always use sharp knives*. Blunt knives slip. Cutting yourself hurts and makes you cry. So, Team – first rule of the kitchen is sharp knives, please!

Second rule of the kitchen is *always wash fruit and vegetables* under cold, running water before using them, as they'll most likely have been sprayed with chemicals.

Third rule – OK, these rules are getting a bit much, but we don't want to poison anyone, so just a couple more! The third rule is *always wash your hands* before cooking – and during cooking if they get very dirty or sticky – because no one wants your pesky germs.

Clean work surfaces, dishcloths and towels too. You can spread germs very easily in a kitchen, so keeping everyone and everything sparklingly clean is a very good thing. And remember – clean up when you have finished!

Lastly . . . yes, really, last one! Some things can be quite dangerous in a kitchen – hot, sharp, steamy, slippery, heavy – so *always ask an adult for help* rather than risking it yourself.

✸ **USING THE OVEN** Be especially careful when using the oven. Always use oven gloves and have a clear, heat-proof area ready to lay the item on you are bringing out of the oven. *Always ask an adult to help, if you are unsure.*

✸ **COOKING PASTA** Every bag of pasta you buy will have cooking instructions, but knowing how and why is very helpful when you're starting your cooking life. The trick is to use plenty of boiling, salted water and to stir the pasta occasionally to stop it all sticking together. Why salt, you may ask? Because pasta and gnocchi don't have any added salt, so when you put them into the water the pasta soaks it up, adding flavour and making it soft. Some people like pasta very soft, while others like to chew a bit. This is known as *al dente* in Italy, which is how they like their pasta (it means 'to the tooth' in

English). You can decide how you like yours by carefully lifting a piece from the water a few minutes before it's ready, letting it cool a little, then tasting it.

Two more little things:
1. Never overcook pasta – it's not good soggy.
2. Always have the sauce ready before the pasta is cooked. Pasta doesn't like waiting for sauce, just like dogs don't like waiting for their dinner!

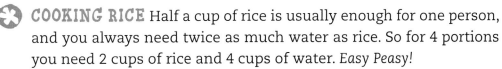 **COOKING RICE** Half a cup of rice is usually enough for one person, and you always need twice as much water as rice. So for 4 portions you need 2 cups of rice and 4 cups of water. *Easy Peasy!*

Put the rice into a sieve and rinse it under cold water to get rid of any starch and impurities. Now, put some water in a saucepan and add enough salt so the water tastes salty. Bring it to the boil on the stove. Carefully, add the rice – don't splash yourself. Give it a stir and bring the water back to a *simmer*. Lower the heat, put the saucepan lid on and cook for 10–15 minutes, or according to the packet instructions. Turn off the heat and let the rice finish cooking in its own steam for another 5 minutes or so. When you take the lid off, the rice will have soaked up the water and the grains will be separated and soft. You can fluff it up with a fork.

. . . .

BEWARE!
Cooked rice should not be kept. Best to eat it all once you've cooked it.

. . . .

COOKING ROOT VEGETABLES Root vegetables grow underground – potatoes, carrots, swedes, beetroot, parsnips. They should always be washed and scrubbed and put into cold, salted water for cooking. The water should cover the vegetables by a centimetre or two.

✿ **COOKING GREEN VEGETABLES** Green vegetables cook quickly and should always be added to a saucepan of boiling water. Wash and trim any stalks or damaged leaves. If you're eating green vegetables cold, refresh them under cold water straight away when they're cooked and drained. This keeps them looking bright and tasting firm.

✿ **NEARLY COOKED**

Potatoes – Push the pointed end of a knife into a couple of potatoes while they're still in the pot to see how firm they are. If the knife slides in easily, they're ready. If it still feels a bit firm, then they're 'nearly cooked'!

✿ **IS IT COOKED THROUGH?**

Chicken – You must be very careful to make sure chicken is cooked properly because undercooked chicken has nasty bacteria that could make you poorly. The best way to test if it's ready is to stick the pointed end of a sharp knife into the thickest part of the chicken. If the juice that comes out is pink, then it needs more cooking. Test again after another ten minutes. DON'T EAT PINK CHICKEN!

✿ **CRACKING AN EGG** Have a bowl ready. Whack the egg around its middle on the edge of the bowl, push both thumbs into the crack and let the egg drop from the shell into the bowl. If you bash it too hard, it'll just pour over your hands. A quick, firm whack and into the bowl. Fish out any bits of shell with a spoon or your fingers.

✿ **SEPARATING EGGS** It's messy! You need two bowls. Do exactly what you did for *cracking an egg* but don't let the egg drop into the bowl. Instead, carefully prize apart the two halves, keeping the yolk inside one half and letting the white fall into one of the bowls. Then, very gently, tip the yolk into the other side of the shell, allowing more of the white to drip into the bowl. Keep doing this until you've got most of the white safely in one of the bowls. You never get it all, but you'll get most of it.

✿ **BEATING EGG WHITES** It's easy and fun, *but* when you're separating the eggs to get the whites, you mustn't let even a tiny drop of yolk fall into the whites otherwise they won't whip into pillow-soft clouds of loveliness. Using a hand beater or a whisk and a strong arm, start beating on a low speed for about a minute. Turn up the speed and keep beating until you get those pillow clouds. THE TEST! Are you ready for this? Turn the bowl upside down and if the egg whites stay put, they're perfect. If you need a shower, they're not!

✿ **MELTING BUTTER** This simply means putting the butter into a bowl and heating in the microwave for a few seconds at a time. Keep checking, so it doesn't spit everywhere. The other way is to put the butter in a small pan, over a low heat, and let it melt slowly. Don't let it go brown because burnt butter is disgusting.

✿ **PEEL & SLICE**
Onions – Using a sharp knife, take a thin slice off the top and bottom. Use your fingers and peel away the papery skin. You may find it easier to cut the onion in half before peeling it. *Slicing* means cutting through the peeled onion half as thinly or as thickly as the recipe asks for. If you're asked to 'chop' it, then just slice the onion into wedges and chop up the wedges.
Garlic – Peel the garlic by taking a thin slice off the top and bottom. You can use whole, peeled cloves or chop and slice them. If you need to use a garlic crusher, just pop the peeled clove in and squeeze till the juicy bits ooze out.
Carrot – Using a sharp knife, take a thin slice off the top and bottom. With a vegetable peeler, peel from the top to the bottom and keep turning the carrot until it's done. Now, rinse under cold, running water.

TOP & TAIL This simply means taking a small slice off the top and the bottom of the fruit or vegetable you're using.

Spring onions – These are just like tiny leeks. All you need to do is cut off some of the dark green leaves, then take a small slice off the bottom – the white bit. If some of the outer white skin looks loose, just peel it off. If they're dirty, rinse them under cold, running water.

DE-SEED & SLICE

Peppers – Slice off the stalk end and pull the pepper in half. Tap out all the little white seeds and pull off any white fleshy bits. That's it, ready for slicing, chopping or eating raw!

PEEL & CORE

Apples – Begin by cutting the apple in half and then quarters. Carefully cut out the hard core and pips in the centre of each quarter. Then peel the quarters. It's quite difficult, so you may need some help at first. Apples tend to go brown if they're not used quite quickly after peeling, so only peel them when you're ready to use them.

STONING FRUIT This means taking out the large stone in the middle of a peach, plum, avocado or anything else that has a stone in it, before cooking! Hold the fruit firmly down on the work surface and, with your sharp knife, cut all the way around the middle. Now twist the two halves in opposite directions and they'll come apart. One half will have the stone still in it, so just pull it out. Sometimes they don't want to come, so be firm. Show them who's boss!

Mangoes – We find the best way is to slice through the skin, from top to bottom, about four times – more if the mango is not very ripe. Then dig your fingers into the top of one of the slices and carefully peel away the skin. Now carefully, because mangoes are very slippery without their skins, slice away the flesh. The stone inside a mango is huge, so watch out for it; you'll hit it sooner than you think. Just

get as much of the flesh off as you can and give the stone to the birds to finish off!

✳ **GRATED RIND & JUICE** You can grate the rind of an orange, lemon or lime. Rub the fruit up and down on a grater until all the 'zest' has come off. Careful of your fingers, though – graters are sharp. When you've removed the rind/zest, cut the fruit in half and either use your hands to squeeze out the juice or find a squeezer in the cutlery drawer. Ask for some help, if you need it. If you warm the fruit first, either in a bowl of hot water for a couple of minutes or in the microwave for a minute, you'll find it easier to squeeze.

✳ **TOASTING NUTS & SEEDS** The smell of toasted nuts and seeds is divine. There are lots of ways to do it:

1. Put them on a plate in the microwave and cook on high for about 30 seconds. Keep doing that until they start to brown and smell wonderful.

2. Heat a dry frying pan and when hot, tip in the seeds or nuts and give them a stir. They're ready when they start to brown and smell good. Tip them out of the frying pan, otherwise they'll go on cooking and might burn.

3. If the oven is already on, pop them on a baking tray and roast for about 5 minutes. Check they're ready using your nose and eyes!

. . . .

WARNING!
Nuts and seeds burn really quickly and taste horrible. So keep checking them and never leave them alone!

. . . .

✳ **KNEADING** The recipes in this book only suggest a little bit of kneading, which is good news for small hands. Sprinkle the work surface and your hands with a little flour. Tip the dough out onto the flour and, using the heel of your hand (that's the flat bit attached to your wrist!), push down into the dough and away from you. Fold the dough over, anyway you like, and do the same again. Keep doing this until the dough feels like the recipe says it should. If you have a food processor, use that. It'll take a few minutes at most on a medium speed.

 **MARINADING** This is a way of adding flavour to food and making it more tender, or softer to eat, before cooking. You can marinade meat, fish, chicken, vegetables or tofu. You've probably seen stuff going on the BBQ that's been marinaded. A marinade is usually a liquid or sauce which allows the food to soak up flavours before cooking it.

SWEET & SOUR We suggest sea salt in all the recipes, as it is more flavoursome and you can use less. When we suggest using a little sugar or honey to adjust the flavour of a dish, use as little as possible. The less sweetness in your food, the less sugar you will want.

SIMMER Generally, once you've brought something to the boil (and it's bubbling like a volcano!), you turn down the heat until there are just tiny, little fizzy bubbles on the surface. That's simmering!

TINS In these recipes use 425g tins. Tinned beans and chickpeas are kept in salty water. This should be drained off in a sieve or colander and the pulses rinsed in cold water befoore using.

The Last Word

So, there you have it!

Either you've just worked your way through every recipe and successfully cooked them all, or you've opened this book on the last page to see what this cooking lark is all about! Either way, we're all on the same page – so to speak. We all enjoy eating tasty, good stuff and sharing it with friends. Cooking the *Easy Peasy* way makes it all possible.

You already know that practice makes perfect. Think about it. You didn't know how to walk until you stood up and put one foot in front of the other. It was that first step that set you off. Reading, writing? Well, it took a few years to learn but, hey, look how good you are at it now. Learning to cook and loving what you make is exactly the same deal.

Take that first step. Cut your first carrot, stir your first sauce, and before you can say 'fry an egg' you'll be a confident cook with a drawer full of skills and ideas ready to do your own thing. You can do it!

You can eat what you like. You can cook for your pals. You can eat well, cut the rubbish and have great fun. Job done!

So, take it from us, learning to cook is like riding a bike! Once you've got it, you've got it for life. Well done, you!

Much love,

Easy & Peasy xxx

139

Acknowledgements

Our thanks to all at Birlinn, especially Jan Rutherford, Andrew Simmons, Deborah Warner and Abigail Salvesen. Thanks to Jim Hutcheson, for the *Easy Peasy* cover and design, and Mark Blackadder for the page layout. And thanks to Ruth Armstrong for her brilliant photography. Thanks to all the *Easy Peasy* cooks who cooked, helped photograph and ate the recipes, and the team at Valvona & Crolla for all their help.

Index

apples
    Bramley apples 130
    Granny Smith 123
    More Fruits . . . 127
    peeling and coring 136
almonds
    nut burger 108
    Crunchy, Nutty, Sweet and Salty 70
apricots 127
avocado 25
    removing stone 136

bacon
    egg and bacon muffins 49
    lardons (bacon bits) 30, 49, 112
bananas 18, 67, 77, 124
beans
    cannellini 112
    green beans 106
    kidney 98
beef (minced) 50, 98
beetroot 38
blackberries 67
blueberries 67
bread 58, 59, 64, 91
    breadcrumbs 37, 57, 60, 62, 63, 64, 108, 109, 116
    crusty bread 83, 96, 117
    damper (Australian soda bread) 26
    flatbread 11, 20, 22, 25, 41, 45, 53, 85, 95, 99
    pitta bread 19, 22

burgers
    Burger Buns 50
    nut burger 108
    Portobello Burgers 36
    Turkey Burgers 34
butter, melting 135

cakes and cookies
    cheese scones 17
    cookies 72
    fruit scones 16–17
    plain scones 17
    sables 14
carrots 38, 84
    Carrot Hummus 21
    Moorish Carrot Salad 84
    peeling and slicing 135
cauliflower 46
cheese 49, 60, 65
    Cheesy Easy Peasy Pasta 29
    feta 87
    mascarpone 81
    Parmasan 24, 32
    mozzarella 121
    sables 14
    scones 17
chia seeds 127, 130
chicken 45, 62
    checking for 'cooked through' 134
    curry 94
    in soup 54
    Lemon Chicken and Potato Wedges 100
    noodles 106

chickpeas 19, 40
cleanliness, need for 132
coconut milk 18, 74
cookies 72
courgettes 108
    Courgette Chips 23
croutons 31, 90, 91
cucumber 88
curry (Tutti Frutti Chicken) 94

dips
    Pea, Parsley and Mint Dip 13
    hummus 20
    Carrot Hummus 21
    Green Pea Hummus 20
    rocket pesto 24
drinks
    berry smoothie 67
    Chai Latte 74
    Pink Drink 78
    soya smoothie 77

eggs
    beating egg whites 135
    cracking of 134
    Egg and Bacon Muffins 49
    Eggy Pots 65
    Mozzarella Eggs 121
    separating eggs 134–5
    Spanish Omelette 96

falafel 40
feta cheese 87
fish
    salmon fillets 119
flatbread 11
fruit
    grating rind 137
    squeezing for juice 137
    stoning fruit 136
    washing fruit 132

fruit scones 16–17

garlic, peeling and slicing 135
ginger 74, 104, 124
gnocchi 110–11
    sauce for 114–15
goat's milk 74
green vegetables, cooking of 134

herbs
    basil 32, 60, 83, 114
    bay leaves 119
    coriander 21, 25, 34, 40, 47,
        70, 99
    dill 88
    mint 13, 30
    parsley 13, 46, 53, 84, 87
    rosemary 60, 100
    thyme 60, 100
hummus 19
    Carrot Hummus 21
    Green Pea Hummus 20

ice cream 81
ice cubes 78

kneading 137–8
    flatbreads 11
koftas (spiced meatballs) 102–3

lamb (minced) 102
lardons (bacon bits) 30, 49, 112
lemons 13, 19, 20, 21, 24, 25, 34, 45,
        100
    grating rind 137
    lemon juice 81, 84, 87, 90
lunchbox treats 39, 42, 93, 97, 109

mangoes 18
    removing stone of 136–7
maple syrup 67, 68

marinading 138
    tofu 120
mascarpone (soft Italian cream
    cheese) 81
muesli 128
mozzarella 121
muffins
    Egg and Bacon Muffins 49
mushrooms
    chestnut mushrooms 53
    Portobello mushrooms 36

noodles 106
nuts
    flaked almonds 46, 70, 123, 128,
        129
    nut burger 108–9
    pine nuts 24, 32
    snack spicy nuts 70–1
    toasting nuts and seeds 137
    walnuts 123

oats
    Coconut Milk Porridge 18
    Marvellous Muesli 128
    So Soya Smoothie 77
olives 87
onions
    peeling and slicing 135
    spring onions 42, 54, 106
oranges 124
    fresh orange juice 18, 21, 78
    grating rind and juicing 137
    ice cream 81
    unsweetened orange juice 123, 127

pancakes 68
parsnips 38
pasta
    Cheesy Easy Peasy Pasta 29
    cooking pasta 132

Soo-go (tomato pasta sauce) 114,
    117
peaches 123, 127
    removing stone of 136
peanut butter 21
pears 127, 128
peas
    Green Pea Hummus 20
    Pea, Parsley and Mint Dip 13
    Beautiful Pea Green Boat
        (soup) 30
    petits pois 20
peeling
    apples 136
    carrots 135
    garlic 135
    onions 135
peppers 83
    de-seeding and slicing 136
    green pepper 104, 106, 108
    red pepper 98
    yellow pepper 93
pesto
    basil pesto 32
    rocket pesto 24
picnic treats
    corn critters 42
    falafel 40
    flatbreads 11
    hummus 19, 20, 21
    nut burgers 108
    sables 14
    Spanish omelette 96
plums 123
    removing stone of 136
pork 104, 116
potatoes
    checking for 'nearly cooked' 134
    creamy mashed potatoes 56
    lemon wedges 101
    new potatoes 96

pumpkin 60–1
    pumpkin seeds 61

raspberries 78
rhubarb 124
rice, cooking 133
rocket 24
root vegetables, cooking of 133

sables 14
salads
    Caesar salad 90
    cucumber salad 88
    feta salad 87
    carrot salad 84
    roast pepper salad 83
salmon 119
sauces
    sugo tomato sauce 114
sausages
    beans and 112
    chorizo sausage 93
sesame seed paste (tahini) 19, 20, 21
shortcrust pastry 93
simmer 138
smoothies
    banana and oat 77
    berry blue soya smoothie 67
soups
    chicken and sweetcorn 54
    Beautiful Pea Green Boat 30
soya milk 67, 77
soya yoghurt 77
spices
    cardamom 18, 74

cayenne pepper 84
chilli flakes 40, 53, 98, 102, 112
cinnamon 70, 74, 98, 127
cloves 70
cumin 20, 21, 34, 40, 47, 84, 98
curry powder 94
harissa (chilli paste) 84
paprika 38, 84
spinach 24, 97
spring onions
    Chow-Chow Noodles 106
    Corn Critters 42
    Chicken and Sweetcorn Soup 54
    topping and tailing 136
squash 60
strawberries 78, 127, 130
sugo tomato sauce 114
    meatballs in 116
    on pizza base 114
sultanas 16, 94, 127, 128
sweetcorn 42, 54

tofu 120
tomatoes 25, 36, 87, 94, 98, 102, 112, 114
    sugo tomato sauce 114
    on toast (à la Eric) 58
turkey 34

vegetables
    green vegetables, cooking of 134
    root vegetables, cooking of 133

watercress 24